A TAPESTRY OF
GRACE

REFLECTIONS FROM OUR JOURNEY

SIDE BY SIDE - PITTSBURGH

urbanpress

COPYRIGHT/LICENSURE

Book Cover: Cover Photography by Sarah Cudney Photography
www.sarahcudneyphotography.com
Cover Loom Artist: Tammy L. Deck of TLD Designs www.tlddesigns.com
Graphic Design: Shillika Chandrasekhar for cover and editorial design

COPYRIGHT INFORMATION

Oceans (Where Feet May Fall)

Lord I Need You

Writer(s): Christy Nockels, Daniel Carosn, Jesse Reeves, Kristian Stanfill, Matt Maher

Your Hands

Writer(s): David and JJ Heller.

He's Always Been Faithful

Writer(s): New Words & Music by Sara Groves, based on "Great is Thy Faithfulness" by Thomas O. Chisholm & William M. Runyan.

Even when it Hurts

Writer(s): Joel Houston

Eye of the Storm

Writer(s): Bryan Fowler, Ryan Stevenson Label Copy:

Broken Vessels (Amazing Grace)

Writer(s): Joel Houston, Jonas Myrin

Blessings

Writer(s): Laura Story

Resurrecting

Writer(s): Chris Brown/Mack Brock/Steven Furtick/Wade Joye/Matthews Thabo Ntele

My Worth is not it what I Own

Writer(s): Graham Kendrick/Keith Getty/Kristyn Getty

Perfect Wisdom of our God

Writer(s): Keith Getty, Stuart Townend

Trust in You

Writer(s): Lauren Daigle/Michael Farren/Paul Mabury

My Story

Words and Music by Michael Weaver and Jason Ingram

This book is dedicated to all the women and families who have traveled this medical journey with us as part of Side By Side-Pittsburgh, and to sweet Evvy Kautza, Ellis Boone, & Molly Mathew who went ahead of us to heaven.

We can't wait to see you in glory!

CONTENTS

FOREWORD

In 1987, my husband, Tim, announced that he would be leaving the Navy to continue his medical training at Mayo Clinic in Rochester, Minnesota. When I heard his decision for our future, a vision from God came into my mind. That vision was to start a Bible study in this new place. After all, many people from all over the world come to Mayo Clinic for medical training and physical healing—so wouldn't that be the perfect place to tell them about Jesus?

Once we arrived in Rochester, it took me many months to act on that vision and invite women to this "international" Bible study. My sense of inadequacy, rejection, and fear to try something new eroded my confidence to start. I tried joining the women's Bible study at my church, but I did not fit in. The women were all nice, but one said to me, "You are a doctor's wife—you have no problems." Hearing that statement convinced me that she did not understand me or my life.

I decided it was my time to venture out of my comfort zone and act on the vision God gave me. Consequently, I asked five women—all wives of residents who were new to town—to join me for a Bible study in my home. All of them agreed to participate and thus we began learning more about God and loving one another at my kitchen table.

A year later, this little group of residents' wives had grown to number 18. We were then occupying three homes to accommodate the larger number of women and the children they brought in tow. Six months after that, we moved to an even larger space at a welcoming church where we all could meet at the same time and share our childcare expenses. By the time my husband's training was finished, 40 women were attending Side By Side each week.

Many women who came to Side By Side had never previously attended a

Bible study, while others had been in Bible studies all their lives. We found a common bond in the fact that we were all in a healthcare marriage, and provided encouragement, friendship, and support for one another. Side By Side continued to grow and in 2001, a group of insightful women decided that we should be in every medical community across the country. We firmly believed that the model of building God's kingdom and walking alongside women in medical marriages just had to be shared. With this mission in mind, these faithful women began the process of writing down what we did and how and why we did it. We also prayed fervently.

In 2005, we affiliated with the Christian Medical and Dental Association (CMDA) and became their ministry for women who were married to doctors and dentists. Being a part of a larger organization with a solid Christian medical focus and many years of successful management has provided great assistance in our growth.

As I write, we still see God's hand increasing the number of women in Side By Side. Currently there are about 85 chapters, which means 1,324 women in medical marriages are meeting regularly across the country. Three of our Side By Side chapters are outside the United States, supporting women in medical marriages in Japan and Africa. There are also women in medical marriages that are not in our Side By Side chapters. Many of these women receive support from our Facebook group through which 2,100 members communicate and network. In addition, we also send a monthly devotional to an email list of 700. Most important of all, however, the souls of many women, their children, and even their husbands have been won for Christ through the ministry of Side By Side.

In Side By Side, we continue to pray for, love, and encourage one another in our relationships with Christ, our husbands, and our sisters. This is our mission field. We are living it, we understand it, and we have a mighty God who loves us along our way.

The world in which we live believes that woman who are married to a doctors have no problems. That belief is simply not true. We do have problems and we desperately need an understanding community to encourage us along the long path the medical journey requires. This collection of essays from the women in Side By Side-Pittsburgh captures the power of community. As these women share their hearts, minds, and lives, you may recognize your own journey through their words. I challenge you to read and reflect on their stories and find or build a faith community where you can share yours.

Robin W. Morgenthaler
Founder and Executive Director
Side By Side
www.cmda.org/sidebyside (website)
sidebysideinfo@gmail.com (email)

INTRODUCTION

The air in the room felt heavy as our Side By Side group wrapped up discussion for the night.

The evening's study had focused on God's *hesed* love: "Love without an exit." As we prepared to go home, each one of us sat reflecting on how often we have fallen short in showing this type of love as a wife, mother, and friend—the regret in our hearts and minds was palpable. From the silence one woman spoke, "Could we end tonight by reminding ourselves of the gospel?"

Immediately, the weight lifted as we collectively redirected our hearts to Ephesians 2:4-5, "Because of his great love for us, God, who is rich in mercy, made us alive with Christ even when we were dead in transgressions—it is by grace you have been saved." Instead of making resolutions of trying harder to achieve *hesed* love, we remembered what Jesus' *hesed* love achieved for us once and for all through His death and resurrection.

Ephesians 4:15 exhorts believers to "speak the truth in love." Commonly this is interpreted to mean that we are to say hard things in a loving way. Perhaps a better interpretation is that speaking the truth in love calls believers to remind each other of the truth of the gospel. After all, the most loving thing that we can do for a believer caught in sin is to remind them of the redemption that is already secured for them through Christ.

Pastor and author Tim Keller summarizes this beautifully. He says, "The Gospel is this: We are more sinful and flawed in ourselves than we ever dared believe, yet at the very same time we are more loved and accepted in Jesus Christ than we ever dared hope" (2011, page 44). The gospel does not excuse us of our sin, at least not in the sense that it makes sin insignificant. Rather, it reminds us that the infinite penalty for our sin was already paid through death, the death of God's Son on our behalf!

Paradoxically, it is only when we understand the seriousness of our sin that we can understand the good news of the gospel. We are reconciled to God not by any works of our own but because of the work of Jesus on the cross. It was by meditating on this truth that our heavy-hearted Side By Side group received new life! This was the *hesed* "love without an exit" that we all needed to hear.

This book is a collection of essays written by the women in Side By Side-Pittsburgh, a Bible study comprised of women whose husbands are in the medical profession. These pages are filled with stories of joy and pain. They are personal and speak to deep struggles especially present in medical marriages—uprooting families to new cities in order to train or find work, moving far away from family and support systems, the long hours of training and parenting without support, little income during residency, large debt after residency, and the overwhelming loneliness that comes with feeling on our own since others do not understand our situation and circumstances.

At the same time, these stories encompass experiences that are known by all—everyday struggles and fiery trials. Together our group has walked through seasons of infertility, the death of parents, major illnesses, the suicide of siblings, miscarriages, loss of children, abuse, addiction, and career disappointments. Sometimes the grief and pain have been too much to bear. We have often come to God in complete brokenness and surrender, and we have come to one another not to fix each other's pain, but to stand beside one another, side by side. We have offered a shoulder to cry on, a listening ear, and space to grieve. We tell one another, "It's okay to not be okay," and we count on each other to bring our requests before our heavenly Father.

In many ways, our lives are like a tapestry. When we look at the backside of a tapestry, all we see are knots, tangled threads, loose and messy interweaving, and no detail. Often we view our lives from the backside of the tapestry. It's difficult to see the purpose and beauty in the mundane or when we are walking through seasons of suffering. In 1 Corinthians 13:12 Paul wrote, "For now we see in a mirror dimly, but then face to face. Now I know in part; then I shall know fully, even as I have been fully known." We may never know the purpose or beauty on this side of heaven, but one day we will see the full tapestry in all its glory. Every strand will expose a detail that was once unclear or unknown.

We are grateful God has woven our lives together for a season in His beautiful tapestry. Many of us now live far away from each other, but the common threads of our journey and faith continue to bind us together. Above all we have been through together, we are grateful for the thread of God's grace, the free and unmerited favor of God that saves and sustains us. The tapestry of our lives is one of underserved grace.

In 2 Corinthians 1:3-7, Paul wrote,

> Blessed be the God and Father of our Lord Jesus Christ, the Father of mercies and God of all comfort, who comforts us in all our affliction, so that we may be able to comfort those who are in any affliction, with the comfort with which we ourselves are comforted by God. For as we share abundantly in Christ's sufferings, so through Christ we share abundantly in comfort too. If we are afflicted, it is for your comfort and salvation; and if we are comforted, it is for your comfort, which you experience when you patiently endure the same sufferings that we suffer. Our hope for you is unshaken, for we know that as you share in our sufferings, you will also share in our comfort (ESV).

God comforts us in our trouble so we can comfort others during their time of trouble. We pray that these reflections from our journey will comfort you and strengthen your faith. We have included song lyrics that have impacted us through this journey and encourage you to check out these artists and listen along as you read. We have also included verses so you can reflect on God's Word. God is rich in mercy, and we are sustained by His grace. Speaking the truth in love, we share our stories with you.

i will walk by

FAITH

even if i cannot see

2 CORINTHIANS 5:7

OCEANS (WHERE FEET MAY FAIL)

HILLSONG UNITED

You call me out upon the waters
The great unknown where feet may fail
And there I find You in the mystery
In oceans deep
My faith will stand

And I will call upon Your name
And keep my eyes above the waves
When oceans rise, my soul will rest in Your embrace
For I am Yours and You are mine

Your grace abounds in deepest waters
Your sovereign hand
Will be my guide
Where feet may fail and fear surrounds me
You've never failed and You won't start now

So I will call upon Your name
And keep my eyes above the waves
When oceans rise, my soul will rest in Your embrace
For I am Yours and You are mine

Spirit lead me where my trust is without borders
Let me walk upon the waters
Wherever You would call me
Take me deeper than my feet could ever wander
And my faith will be made stronger
In the presence of my Savior

GROWING IN COMMUNITY

RACHEL SCHREITER

"So if there is any encouragement in Christ, any comfort from love, any participation in the Spirit, any affection and sympathy, complete my joy by being of the same mind, having the same love, being in full accord and of one mind. Do nothing from selfish ambition or conceit, but in humility count others more significant than yourselves. Let each of you look not only to his own interests, but also to the interests of others."

Philippians 2:1-4

Four years ago, I sat in my first Side By Side get together. I was pregnant with my first child and I had no idea what was in store as my husband began his medical residency program. I left that evening with reasons why this group really "wasn't for me." Little did I know how differently I would feel three years later.

We had just finished residency and were starting fellowship. I was in a church lobby in a brand-new city, sans husband, with a rambunctious toddler running about and a baby strapped to my chest. I was heavy with anxiety and exhaustion—we had just moved for the third time in four years, leaving behind any semblance of community. I had just resigned from the only professional job I ever had and left the only church to which I ever felt I belonged.

It was only our second week in this new city, and what was I hearing? A kind woman was encouraging me to come to a Side By Side gathering. This time I listened and I went—and will be forever grateful that I did.

Community is everywhere in Scripture. It existed before any of us did. The Holy Trinity is the most holy community that exists, and it shows us how serious God is about our being in relationship with one another. Given that truth, it doesn't mean being in community is easy or routine. Balancing fellowship, everyday tasks, job responsibilities, and time alone is different for all of us.

In those three years of residency, I had an imbalance of too much time alone and not enough time spent with others. What's more, my years walking through medical training with my husband were not the first years I struggled to find fellowship.

At a young age, my father left our family unexpectedly, leaving behind an overwhelming burden that my family still carries. His departure negatively influenced my understanding of relationship at an impressionable age. All too frequently, I believed that I was different and that everyone else had it easier because I was alone. I was fixated on the idea that instead of this past rejection having purpose in my life, it had limited my ability to relate to others socially and spiritually.

Gently and graciously, God revealed to me my mistake—I was wrongly focused on my hurts, what people had to offer me, and all the ways people had hurt me—it was all about me. It was important for me to have the time and space to acknowledge those real areas of pain and mourn my loss. Staying in that place, however, was not helping and believing I was alone was a lie. These thoughts were limiting me, encouraging me to take my focus off God's grace in my life.

It has taken me a long time to understand that my earthly experience has been transformed instead of hindered by my lack of relationships. Jesus' ever-present grace and redemption wove their way into my story long before my father stepped out of our lives. God planted people in every stage of my life to share the gospel, speak truth into my heart, and help me remember the times when Christ was loyally present, unlike the hurtful times important people had failed to be.

When I joined Side By Side-Pittsburgh, it was late summer. By the following winter, I was humbly sitting in awe at the wisdom that surrounded me. These precious women were all amidst the storms of life and were bravely stepping into them in community. My newly-found friends were boldly sharing their hurts, sins, and prayer needs openly—all while their spouses tirelessly worked to support their families and patients with little reinforcement, sleep, or time at home.

Over the course of that next year we spent in that new city, I said yes to more than I usually do. I sometimes pushed back my kids' bedtimes and went to gatherings alone, which meant I was usually dealing with all that comes with being alone. Now that I reflect on that, it all was worth it.

I opened up to others, became vulnerable, and shared my story. I took steps of obedience towards Christ that led to greater healing and a deeper relationship with Him. His strength allowed me to openly seek prayer for areas I had never had the courage to share before. The love of Christ along with the love from my Side By Side-Pittsburgh sisters surrounded my entire being during my involvement with my new family.

Paul wrote in Philippians at the beginning of this devotional that Christ came to serve our needs and not His own. He expects us to do the same. As I moved out of my own pain and took notice of the pain others were in, I had a chance to not just receive healing but also to give it as well. I found I was not the only person with deep needs in the group; I discovered that we all had them! That in itself was liberating, and as I entered into other's sorrows, God continued to heal mine. That was another important lesson from being together with others whom I knew and who knew me.

What I've learned through it all is that God reveals Himself in community. His desire is for us to know Him better and to trust that He has us right where He wants us. God has introduced me to a host of people in my jobs, neighborhoods, and churches who are walking bravely through life's challenges and revealing the opportunity to love without limitation in ways that have gone far beyond my expectations.

God is teaching me to move beyond my self-imposed limitations so I can seek the transformative power of the Holy Spirit, the redeeming grace of Jesus Christ, and the sovereign will of my loving and gracious Father God. I discovered that it takes courage to step out and show up, but once we arrive at that place, the work He is able to do in us is truly magnificent.

REFLECTION & APPLICATION

1. Write a memory when you said yes to being part of a group or community, even though it was challenging. How did God work through this experience or meet you in that experience?

2. What are some biblical examples of godly community or relationships that come to mind? List verses or examples of stories from the Bible.

3. In Philippians 2, Paul directed us to look after the interests of others and not just our own. Where can you apply this command in your church, neighborhood, or workplace? Where have you allowed your own needs to keep you from ministering to others?

4. What are some ways that you can look beyond yourself and focus on others? Why not step out of your comfort zone this week and set up a time to "have coffee" with someone as a first step toward building community with others?

Father, thank You that You reveal Yourself through community. I pray that You will provide relationships that encourage me in my faith and point me to Christ. Help me to see Your provision through the people You have placed in my life and help me to know and serve You more fully because of these relationships.

Rachel Schreiter and her husband, Ryan, live outside of Philadelphia, PA. Rachel is currently at home with their two children and pursuing a masters in biblical counseling. Ryan is a physician at Temple University, practicing non-operative sports medicine. Rachel was part of Side By Side-Pittsburgh from 2015 to 2016.

rejoice always

PRAY

without ceasing

1 THESSALONIANS 5:16-17

LORD, I NEED YOU

MATT MAHER

Lord, I come, I confess
Bowing here I find my rest
Without You I fall apart
You're the One that guides my heart

Lord, I need You, oh, I need You
Every hour I need You
My one defense, my righteousness, Oh God, how I need You

Where sin runs deep Your grace is more
Where grace is found is where You are
And where You are, Lord, I am free
Holiness is Christ in me

Lord, I need You, oh, I need You
Every hour I need You
My one defense, my righteousness, Oh God, how I need You

To teach my song to rise to You
When temptation comes my way
When I cannot stand I'll fall on You
Jesus, You're my hope and stay

Lord, I need You, oh, I need You
Every hour I need You
My one defense, my righteousness, Oh God, how I need You
You're my one defense, my righteousness, Oh God, how I need You

IN QUIETNESS AND TRUST

RACHAEL LEUENBERGER

---

*"In returning and rest you shall be saved, in quietness
and in trust shall be your strength."*

Isaiah 30:15

"Maybe we should pray," my two-year old said with gentle confidence. Nearby, her fellow diaper-wearing companion was struggling to poop, a situation requiring immediate intercession in my daughter's mind. Every adult within earshot chuckled.

In the moment, laughter was the natural response, but I knew that her prayer was sincere. We had been frequently employing prayer with our daughter as she struggled with constipation, and so it was natural for her to suggest we pray for her friend. Our daughter was learning to trust in the Lord's power and delight to intercede on her behalf. It is to this same childlike faith we are all called, even as grown-up believers.

We live in an age and culture that are exceedingly prosperous, resource-rich, and educated. Our technological advancements have reached beyond what those a century before could imagine. Our life expectancy has continually increased, leaving us to ignore thoughts of our mortality. Our access to resources through our affluence has caused us to glorify our self-sufficiency more than ever before. It is this culture that makes the concept of trusting the Lord so foreign to our hearts.

Rather than leave our cares in the hands of the One who created the universe and delicately knit us together, instead we place our trust in our achievements, education, wealth, and power. How much greater is this temptation for those of us immersed in the achievement-oriented culture of medicine?

Our family is in a tough season of parenting as we do the hard work of caring for three kids who are four and under. When we encounter a trial, our first reflex is to turn to Google and the opinions of others. Then we triage the advice we receive and create a battle plan: First A, then B, and that brings us to C. Unfortunately, prayer and seeking wisdom from God's word typically fall under E or F in our plans. As our kids grow and the parenting challenges (and conundrums) increase, we find ourselves increasingly weary.

In our brokenness, one Sunday our pastor preached from a passage in Isaiah 30 that rekindled our desire to confidently trust the Lord. In that chapter, the Israelites were frightened by the aggressive Assyrians and took refuge in the swift horses and power of the Egyptian army. As Israel looked to Egypt to be their salvation, they forgot the Lord—their Protector who was in covenant relationship with them. Instead, they trusted in the passing powers of this world.

This struggle is a familiar one today. Like Israel, we trust in the power and security of the answers the world offers. We rest in the good things the Lord has given while failing to worship Him as the source of our salvation. The swift horses of Egypt's army were not inherently bad, and neither are the gifts God gives today. Resting in their power, however, can become idolatrous.

In Isaiah 30:15, the Lord speaks, saying, "In returning and rest you shall be saved, in quietness and in trust shall be your strength." The command is to take our eyes off the things of this world and return to our dependence on God for salvation and strength. Quiet trust inverts our battle plan; prayer becomes first and foremost.

At times, this plan feels passive. Certainly an active pursuit through a systematic approach feels most beneficial when we encounter trials. To do this in the absence of prayer, however, puts the sufficiency solely on us, which will lead to certain failure. Instead, we must acknowledge that we cannot produce meaningful change in our own lives, the lives of others, or our broken world apart from the power of God. Though God may choose to work through education, wealth, achievement, or Google, when we begin with prayer, we recognize that these things are from Him as well. What a sweet rest we are promised when we shift our dependence from ourselves to God!

REFLECTION & APPLICATION
1. Describe a time in your life when first taking a situation to the Lord in prayer changed your approach or altered your heart towards the problem.

2. What biblical stories or examples come to your mind when thinking about the power of prayer? What lessons did you learn from these examples?

3. Read 1 Thessalonians 5:16-18. We are encouraged to "pray without ceasing." What distracts you and takes away from being able to do this?

4. Write a prayer about something that is currently challenging for you. How can you actively put your trust in the Lord for that situation as opposed to the advice the world would give of how that could be resolved? Challenge yourself to seek God's guidance in this matter and to wait patiently for His response.

Father, may I enter the sweet rest that You offer as I learn to shift my dependence from myself to You. Help me take my eyes away from the fleeting powers of this world and instead allow me to quiet my heart through prayer. In quietness and trust, I move forward, embracing the hard work you have set before me today.

Rachael Leuenberger has been married to Andy for almost ten years. They were married after Andy's first year of medical school and added three children during his residency and shortly thereafter. Andy works as a family medicine doctor on the South Side of Pittsburgh. They share a mutual hobby of running and a not-so-mutual hobby of knitting. Rachael has been attending Side By Side-Pittsburgh since 2012.

be *joyful* in HOPE
patient in AFFLICTION
faithful in PRAYER

ROMANS 12:12 (NIV)

YOUR HANDS

JJ HELLER

I have unanswered prayers
I have trouble I wish wasn't there
And I have asked a thousand ways
That you would take my pain away
You would take my pain away

I am trying to understand
How to walk this weary land
Make straight the paths that crooked lie
Oh Lord, before these feet of mine
Oh Lord, before these feet of mine

When my world is shaking, heaven stands
When my heart is breaking, I never leave your hands

When you walked upon the earth
You healed the broken, lost and hurt
I know you hate to see me cry
One day you will set all things right
Yeah, one day you will set all things right

When my world is shaking, heaven stands
When my heart is breaking, I never leave your hands

Your hands that shaped the world
Are holding me
They hold me still

14

UNANSWERED PRAYERS (PART 1)

KRISTA CHAMBERS

"Answer me when I call, O God of my righteousness!
You have given me relief when I was in distress."

Psalm 4:1

I was blessed to be raised in a home where we prayed. My parents taught me to love and trust God in all circumstances of my life, and modeled how to do both. We prayed together and we prayed for one another. Before we ate, went to bed, had a big test at school, or a decision to make, we prayed. We prayed when we were sick and we prayed with thanksgiving when we were healthy. I learned at a young age to cry out to God and believed that God would hear and answer my prayers. Consequently, when I was 27 and felt like my life plans were unraveling, I prayed.

It was baby season all around me when I first received the news. My friends and I had journeyed through a season of weddings; now it was time for baby showers and all things pink and blue. My diagnosis brought my dream of having many children to a screeching halt. The injustice that I felt over my diagnosis was almost paralyzing. I felt completely isolated in my pain. My husband and I did not share our struggle with many people, and in the months and years that followed, I sat through countless baby showers praying that God would replace my jealousy, fear, and self-pity with joy for my friends.

I clung to the hope that God would answer my prayer and one day let me join my friends in motherhood. At some point, my husband advised me to stop reading all the books, blogs, and articles about infertility and just trust that God would work it out in His time, and that is what we did. We focused on

God, our marriage, and our careers.

After four years, we decided it was time to meet with a fertility specialist. This was a humbling decision for us, and I was anxious. I constantly questioned my faith. Why had God not answered our prayers yet? How would this all work out? How could we possibly afford fertility treatment when our health insurance did not cover any of it and my husband was only halfway through dental school? How would I be able to make it to all the doctor's appointments with my full-time teaching job—with an hour long commute? It was all too much. The compulsive planner in me couldn't handle it. Many of my friends had planned this part of their life: when to start a family, how many children to have, even the exact month spacing between siblings. They could do all that, but I could not—it was all out of my hands and in God's hands. I knew my anxiety was not going to help me fight this infertility, but prayer would.

Until we made the decision to see a fertility specialist, most of our friends, colleagues, and even families did not know that we had been unable to get pregnant. Infertility is far more common than anyone may think (one in eight couples). Many choose to remain silent about their struggle because it is so personal, intimate, and difficult to talk about. Even though I was nervous to be honest and share with others, we desperately needed a support network. My husband and I decided we could not embark on this unknown journey without prayers and support from family and friends. We began to tell people.

I still struggled with doubt and anxiety, but something significant had shifted—we were no longer alone. Friends helped with logistics like putting together lessons plans for my substitutes, or helping to make sure our prescription meds were received and refrigerated. On days when my anxiety threatened to overwhelm my faith, I often felt God's peace. We had a prayer team of friends and family who were faithfully praying for us.

Through it all, God really taught us the importance of being vulnerable with our struggle and being open to share our story with others. With so much company, we kept going, step-by-step, day-by-day, prayer-by-prayer, as God transformed our vulnerability into something beautiful and sustaining.

REFLECTION & APPLICATION

1. Reflect on a time when you had to earnestly seek God in prayer. How were you affected by this?

2. Is it possible that struggling with God is part of the process for spiritual growth?

3. The Bible is full of examples of faithful servants of God who struggled and cried out to Him: Noah, Abraham, Isaac, Jacob, Sarah, Hagar, David, Hannah, and Job, just to name a few. Reflect on some of their stories. How did they grow through struggle?

4. Read Psalm 34. What verses encouraged you and why?

5. Read Psalm 117:2. As a child of God, you can count on His love and faithfulness to help and sustain you in every situation. Can you think of some times in the past when God has been with you?

Father, thank You for the gift of prayer. I marvel that You, the creator of the universe and sustainer of all things, delights when I come to You with my needs. I thank You also for the community that You have placed in my life: the body of Christ that can uphold me during times of sorrow and waiting.

great is thy faithfulness

LAMENTATIONS 3:23

HE'S ALWAYS BEEN FAITHFUL

SARA GROVES

Great is thy faithfulness, Lord, unto me

Morning by morning I wake up to find
The power and comfort of God's hand in mine
Season by season I watch Him, amazed
In awe of the mystery of His perfect ways
All I have need of, His hand will provide
He's always been faithful to me

I can't remember a trial or a pain
He did not recycle to bring me gain
I can't remember one single regret
In serving God only, and trusting His hand
All I have need of, His hand will provide
He's always been faithful to me

This is my anthem, this is my song
The theme of the stories I've heard for so long
God has been faithful, He will be again
His loving compassion, it knows no end
All I have need of, His hand will provide
He's always been faithful, He's always been faithful
He's always been faithful to me

IN GOD'S TIME (PART 2)

KRISTA CHAMBERS

"Be still before the Lord and wait patiently for him."

Psalm 37:7

On a hot day in July, I held her in my arms. With tears streaming down both of our faces, my husband and I thanked God with all our hearts. She was beautiful and healthy, and she had been given to us after only one round of fertility treatment. We had our sweet baby girl, the answer to our prayers.

Two years later, we returned to the fertility specialist with the same prayers. We went to the same office, used the same treatment, and were hoping for the same outcomes: a quick pregnancy and a healthy baby. This, however, did not happen. During ten failed cycles of the treatment, I waged a continual war against severe depression that included deep valleys of grief with peaks of fleeting hope. I am glad that during our first pregnancy I had learned to be open with our struggle of infertility, because if I had not, I am not sure I would have endured the next three years.

Eventually, my physician advised a course of treatment I had been dreading: In Vitro Fertilization (IVF). IVF is far more physically invasive. I was nervous about all the shots and drugs I would be putting into my body. IVF was also expensive, and we had no way to afford it—my husband was in the middle of residency training and I had quit my job to stay home with our daughter. Also, I had no idea how I would make all the appointments with my three-year-old daughter in tow. We trusted that God would provide a way and asked our friends to pray.

21

Allowing others to share my pain again resulted in many blessings. Family members helped us financially when our own resources ran out. Friends watched my daughter at a moment's notice so I could attend appointments. When my emotional pain was almost unbearable, I was blessed by home-made dinners, cards, emails, and texts. Sometimes friends simply reminded me that God was with me, that He loved me, and He had a plan for me and my family. At other times, friends would just listen. Most important of all, wise friends would distract me, knowing that I didn't have the strength to talk about another failed cycle.

With so many disappointments, this battle of infertility could have crushed my marriage and my faith, but it did not. I will be honest that there were many moments I felt alone and far from God, but I learned that I could not dwell on the reasons for my situation. There was no justice or hope to be found there. Dwelling on myself led to a downward spiral of self-pity, despair, and depression. "Help me to fix my eyes on You, Jesus" became my prayer, and then my source of peace, hope, and even joy.

Our first IVF cycle failed and we lost that baby the morning my husband had to take step two of his medical boards. This was one of the hardest days of this journey. I could not even lean on my husband for support, since he needed to focus on his exam. I wanted to hide myself away somewhere and cry, but that was not going to happen. I had a day planned to explore a new city with my three-year-old daughter and I was determined to create positive memories that day. God was with me and gave me the strength to put my emotions on hold and make it through the day. My daughter and I ended up having a beautiful day, and when my husband finished his exam, we were able to grieve our loss together.

I strove to keep my eyes on Jesus and to keep praying. He answered my cry. Our second IVF treatment finally worked. At the age of 37, I gave birth to a healthy, beautiful baby boy. It had been a decade since my initial diagnosis and nothing had gone according to my plans. God had answered our prayers in His own time and in His own beautiful way.

REFLECTION & APPLICATION

1. Was there a time in your life that you had to wait for something longer than you wanted to?

2. How did God reveal His plans to you and how did this situation draw you nearer to Him?

3. Read James 5:10-11. Why should we count ourselves blessed to wait on the Lord's timing?

4. The world continually tells us that we deserve to get what we want, when we want it. What benefits do you see from waiting on God's timing?

Father, thank You that You know me intimately and that You hold each of my days in Your hand. Help me to fix my eyes on You and trust that Your timing is good. In the midst of seasons of waiting and trial, may I seek the good work that You have prepared for me to do today.

When Krista Chambers and her husband were married, she believed she was marrying a high school band director. After their first year of marriage, her husband felt led to pursue a career in dentistry. They have resided in Pittsburgh for a decade of medical training (four years of dental school and six years of oral and maxillofacial surgery residency). Krista was also a music teacher prior to staying home to raise her two children. She was part of Side By Side-Pittsburgh from 2012 to 2018.

and by
HIS wounds
we are
healed

ISAIAH 53:5

EVEN WHEN IT HURTS

Take this fainted heart
Take these tainted hands
Wash me in your love
Come like grace again

Even when my strength is lost
I'll praise you
Even when I have no song
I'll praise you
Even when it's hard to find the words
Louder then I'll sing your praise

I will only sing your praise

Take this mountain weight
Take these ocean tears
Hold me through the trial
Come like hope again

Even when the fight seems lost
I'll praise you
Even when it hurts like hell
I'll praise you
Even when it makes no sense to sing
Louder then I'll sing your praise

I will only sing your praise

And my heart burns only for you
You are all, you are all I want
And my soul waits only for you
And I will sing till the morning has come

Lord my heart burns only for you
You are all, you are all I want
And my soul waits only for you
And I will sing till the miracle comes

I will only sing your praise

Even when the morning comes
I'll praise you
Even when the fight is won
I'll praise you
Even when my time on earth is done
Louder then I'll sing your praise

I will only sing your praise

BROKENNESS AND HEALING

KRISTEN KAUTZA

"Your love, Lord, reaches to the heavens, your faithfulness to the skies. Your righteousness is like the highest mountains, your justice like the great deep. You, Lord, preserve both people and animals. How priceless is your unfailing love, O God! People take refuge in the shadow of your wings They feast on the abundance of your house; you give them drink from your river of delights. For with you is the fountain of life; in your light we see light."

Psalm 36:5-9

I started dating my husband in high school, we married after our second year of college, and I became pregnant five months later. I was excited but nervous since we were both still finishing up our bachelor's degrees. During my third trimester, I was put on bedrest for preeclampsia. I am not sure if it was my youth or because it was my first pregnancy, but I was naïve about my condition, which in some ways was my saving grace. I thought, *Everyone has healthy babies, right?*

My daughter Abrielle was born at 35 weeks. She stayed in the NICU for a week due to premature lungs, but then we were able to bring our tiny peanut home. She thrived for the next couple years while I finished my teaching degree and my husband finished school. It was not easy, and there were times when we could barely buy peanut butter and bread, let alone pay the rent. Somehow we made it and came out a loving family of three.

A few years later, I was teaching full-time and my husband was in the midst of medical school when we decided that our four-year-old needed a sibling. We had no trouble getting pregnant and the first trimester went by

28

smoothly. I was no longer a young, naïve, first-time mom, and I was nervous that I would develop preeclampsia again. During my first trimester screening, they found extra fluid on our baby's spinal cord. We underwent multiple tests, and after weeks of waiting, we heard the news we didn't want to hear.

Our baby, a little girl we named Evvy, was diagnosed with a lethal form of skeletal dysplasia. Her chest cavity stopped growing and she would never live outside of my body. Giving birth to Evvy and holding my child, who was already with God, will forever be one of the most difficult days of my life.

I was angry at God for not healing Evvy. I was resentful towards Him and my prayers reflected that: *I shouldn't have to explain to my oldest daughter why we couldn't bring her little sister home with us. I shouldn't have to plan a funeral and bury my child. How could You let this happen to me? I'm a good mom and we have a loving family. I believe in You and have been praying. Why didn't You heal her?* I didn't understand why God let this happen and I built a wall between us.

Six months after having Evvy, I became convinced we needed another child. During my third pregnancy, my physical body was healthy but mentally I was not in a good place. No one could convince me that the baby was okay and that I would not develop preeclampsia again. I didn't trust God because I felt He had already let me down. Our third daughter's birth was free of complications and we were quite happy to bring Amelia home, while at the same time feeling guilty for our happiness because we still missed our baby angel, Evvy.

The same year Amelia was born, my husband matched for his surgical residency in Pittsburgh. I'll admit that I came "kicking and screaming." *What's in Pittsburgh?* After our first month in Pittsburgh, I was lonely. I had two young children, my husband was always working in a demanding surgical residency, and I had no friends. Then one Sunday, the first time visiting a church, a woman behind me told me how much she enjoyed watching my baby girl play with my ear during the service. We started talking, and when she found out why we had moved, she told me about Side By Side-Pittsburgh. To be honest, I wasn't interested in the Bible study but I was desperate for friends. Fortunately, friendships flourished quickly and I was instantly connected with a number of women with whom I shared similar life situations.

My Side By Side-Pittsburgh friends have helped me in so many ways. They have challenged me, shown me God's love through their actions, and hugged me when I cried. Little by little, my walls around my heart started to crumble and I was letting God back in. He had never left me, even when I turned my back on Him.

Looking back now, I can see specific events that He was orchestrating, or as the psalmist wrote, in His light I see light. I developed deeper and closer friendships than I had ever experienced. The first year in Pittsburgh, we struggled financially, but somehow each week we had just enough, even though it didn't make sense how on paper. When I looked for a teaching job, He opened up the doors for me at a wonderful school, and He provided loving daycare we could afford. My goofy and thoughtful girls now go to the school where I teach, and through them and my students, I have been able to meet so many wonderful families. I didn't want to come to Pittsburgh, but now I know this is where God wanted us to be and He has blessed us in many ways.

One of the most difficult lessons I learned through this time of grief and uncertainty was that God allows pain in our lives. It exposes our helplessness apart from Him and drives us to seek His help. I'm not guaranteed a life of ease simply because I'm a Christian. It still hurts to think about Evvy, and I don't think I'll ever understand why I lost my child, but now I can see and rejoice in all the ways He has blessed me. Brokenness is where God can stretch us and grow our faith and enhance our relationship with Him.

With the help and encouragement from my Side By Side-Pittsburgh ladies, my relationship with God is different than it was in the early days of my grief. I have found that I can take refuge in the shadow of His wings any time the need arises. As I continue to mature in my faith and encounter painful situations, my response is not what it was when Evvy was born. I now trust God to carry me through.

REFLECTION & APPLICATION

1. Can you think of a time when your resentfulness towards God was reflected in your prayers?

2. When you are faced with a painful situation beyond your understanding, what Bible verses and stories do you go to that give you comfort?

3. Matthew 5:4 says, "Blessed are those who mourn, for they will be comforted." How has this verse proven true to you? How is it a challenge as well?

4. Has God ever revealed Himself to you through a painful situation? How did He meet you in this matter and draw you near to Him? If you are still in the midst of the pain, challenge yourself to go to Him for comfort and pray to see things through His understanding.

Father, thank You that You never leave our side, even in the darkest trials. I pray that I would not just believe that You are real, but that I would have an intimate relationship with You. May You reveal the eternal hope given to me through the death of Your Son Jesus on the cross.

Kristen Kautza grew up in northern Wisconsin where she married Ben, her high school sweetheart. She became involved with Side By Side-Pittsburgh in 2009 while her husband completed his general surgery residency and now his trauma acute care fellowship. Kristen has been teaching a combined second and third grade class at Pittsburgh Urban Christian School for the past seven years. She is also a mom to two daughters, Abrielle and Amelia.

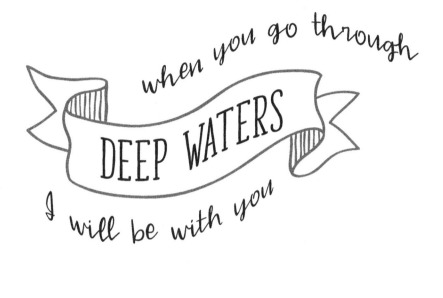

when you go through DEEP WATERS I will be with you

ISAIAH 43:2 (NLT)

EYE OF THE STORM

When the solid ground is falling out
From underneath my feet
Between the black skies and my red eyes, I can barely see
When I realize I've been let down by my friends and my family
I can hear the rain reminding me

In the eye of the storm, You remain in control
In the middle of the war, You guard my soul
You alone are the anchor, when my sails are torn
Your love surrounds, me in the eye of the storm

When my hopes and dreams are far from me
And I'm running out of faith
I see the future I pictured slowly fade away
And when the tears of pain and heartache are pouring down my face
I find my peace in Jesus' name

When they let me go and I just don't know
How I'm gonna make ends meet, I did my best
Now I'm scared to death
That we might lose everything

And when a sickness takes my child away
And there's nothing I can do
My only hope is to trust You, I trust You Lord

In the eye of the storm, You remain in control
In the middle of the war, You guard my soul
You alone are the anchor, when my sails are torn
Your love surrounds me, in the eye of the storm

FAITH IN THE MIDST OF THE STORM

LINDSEY BOONE

"Likewise, the Spirit also helps in our weaknesses. For we do not know what we should pray for as we ought, but the Spirit Himself makes intercession for us with groanings which cannot be uttered. Now He who searches the hearts knows what the mind of the Spirit is, because He makes intercession for the saints according to the will of God."

Romans 8:26-27

I always thought that faithfulness was something I had to achieve on my own—a litmus test for determining if I was a good Christian. It was through a difficult pregnancy and loss of our baby that I realized faithfulness had less to do with me and more to do with the Holy Spirit.

Shortly after learning I was pregnant with identical twin boys at eighteen weeks, we found out that they were growing discordantly. At this point, I became obsessed with reading the medical literature and memorizing statistics regarding outcomes. I spent every extra moment estimating our chances of delivering one or two healthy babies. As our medical complications expanded and we invariably found ourselves in the statistical minority, however, I realized that God doesn't care about statistics. He doesn't fit within the boundaries of human interpretation of probability. What might be a 1% chance for me could be a 100% certainty for Him.

This realization came to me while I was on hospital bedrest trying to prolong our baby's gestation for as long as possible. I decided to give up reading medical literature and eased up questioning my doctors. Instead, I prayed for God to give me faith in Him. That sounds a little strange as

I write it that I needed *Him* to give *me* faith in Him, but I realized I didn't know what it meant to have faith.

One day, our pastor and his wife visited me in the hospital, and I asked them, through tears and sobs, if they thought I had faith. I told them I believed that God could do anything, but didn't expect God should or would do it for me. They informed me my constant prayer and hope in God demonstrated my faith. In that moment, I thought, "Well, who else could I put my hope in?" It seemed obvious that I should turn to God. Medical technology is indeed awesome, but our God is even more so. Medicine has limits, but God does not.

Nobody loves me or knows what I need more than God. On one hand, my doctor would visit me for five minutes in the morning during rounds—I was a summary of numbers and shorthand to him. On the other hand, God was with me every moment of the day, from when I cried at how tiny the baby hats were in the NICU, to when friends emailed me to say they were praying.

Once while sitting alone in a pre-op room and feeling particularly unsettled about our situation, a new nurse walked in to prep me for my procedure. Without any introduction to my background, she looked me straight in the eyes and stated, "God knew that baby in your belly before you did and He is with Him now." I cried grateful tears in response to such a timely statement. God's faithfulness to me in my time of need encouraged me to be faithful to Him. The Spirit knew my weakness and uncertainty about what to pray, but He helped me and was with me every step of the way.

I learned, however, that His faithfulness didn't necessarily mean I get what I wanted. I wanted to deliver two healthy baby boys, but my prayers evolved as our situation changed. One baby died and his brother spent months fighting for his life in the hospital. Because of sin, really bad things happen in this world. Life is not fair. We aren't guaranteed anything on this earth, but God can take the evil and hurt in this world and use it for His glory.

I won't know this side of heaven the ripple effects when we cried out to

Him for six months fighting for the lives of our babies. I do know that process strengthened my faith in Him. I have felt peace in the midst of this storm, knowing that He is in control.

REFLECTION & APPLICATION

1. Write about an event that has challenged and strengthened your faith.

2. List your favorite faith affirming verses or stories that point to trust and reliance in God. How do they move you closer God?

3. Read Hebrews 11, the "great faith chapter." What does it take to please God? What is encouraging to you about this chapter? What is challenging to you about this chapter?

4. Read Psalm 119:30. Faith is a choice. In any situation, we can chose to have faith or to look away from His word and guidance. Are there areas of your life that you need to turn over to God? Write down a list of situations that invoke anxiety or fear and write your own prayer, including verses in Hebrews 11 that you can look to when your faith is challenged.

Father, increase my faith in You. Thank You that You aren't bound by human statistics and the medical advancements or limitations of this world. May I increasingly put my hope in You and be comforted as I remember that You are indeed in control.

Lindsey Boone was with Side By Side-Pittsburgh from 2009 until 2018 while her husband completed general surgery residency and a surgical oncology fellowship. She joined Side By Side in 2009 while working as a postdoc in regenerative medicine but now stays home with her four little boys.

His mercies
are new

EVERY MORNING

LAMENTATIONS 3:23

BROKEN VESSELS (AMAZING GRACE)

HILLSONG WORSHIP

All these pieces
Broken and scattered
In mercy gathered
Mended and whole
Empty handed
But not forsaken
I've been set free
I've been set free

Amazing grace
How sweet the sound
That saved a wretch like me
I once was lost
But now I'm found
Was blind but now I see

Oh I can see you now
Oh I can see the love in Your eyes
Laying yourself down
Raising up the broken to life

You take our failure
You take our weakness
You set Your treasure
In jars of clay
So take this heart, Lord
I'll be Your vessel
The world to see
Your life in me

Amazing grace
How sweet the sound
That saved a wretch like me
I once was lost
But now I'm found
Was blind but now I see

Oh I can see you now
Oh I can see the love in Your eyes
Laying yourself down
Raising up the broken to life

HITTING ROCK BOTTOM (PART 1)

REENA MCCORMICK

"I'll never forget the trouble, the utter lostness, the taste of ashes, the poison I've swallowed. I remember it all—oh, how well I remember—the feeling of hitting the bottom. But there's one other thing I remember, and remembering, I keep a grip on hope: God's loyal love couldn't have run out, his merciful love couldn't have dried up. They're created new every morning. How great your faithfulness! I'm sticking with God (I say it over and over). He's all I've got left."

Lamentations 3:19-24 *The Message*

This past year, I clung to these verses in Lamentations as I cried out to God for new mercies each morning. I tasted the ash and the poison; I had hit rock bottom and God was all I had left. Depression was not a new phenomenon to me. I have struggled on and off with depression for most of my adult life. Up until recently, it had been four years since my last major bout and this time, I was scared. A series of events led me to a state of despair, and I began to have suicidal thoughts. I needed to get help.

The stigma associated with mental illness is paralyzing. Within some Christian circles, depression is considered a sin or a sign of insufficient faith. This causes many of us who struggle with depression not to talk about or hide the issues we are facing. When someone has suicidal thoughts, however, they are not thinking clearly. They truly believe the world, their family, and their friends would be much better off without them. I believed this more times than I would like to admit during my struggles.

If you are not already aware, we have a broken system when it comes to helping people with mental illness. Resources, services, and medical professionals are stretched thin. It was a battle in itself to find help—there was just so much red tape. Doctors weren't taking new patients, clinics were saturated and only open to the uninsured. I made dozens of phone calls and was getting nowhere. I was able to see a therapist I had worked with in the past and, after several months, I finally got a call back from an outpatient intensive program. I began group and individual therapy three days a week, three hours a day, for three months. If you would have asked me before, I would have said there was no way I would ever do a program like this, but I couldn't put my family through this misery any longer. I knew I needed to learn skills to help me cope with my emotions, but I also knew true healing would only come from the Lord.

I wish I could tell you that going through the program was great, but it wasn't. It was one of the hardest and most painful seasons of my life. I felt like I was being broken into a million little pieces and I didn't know if I would ever be put back together. I wrestled with God daily. Where was He? Would He ever heal me? Why did this happen again? Why was I suffering? And how could such a big God love someone as insignificant as me?

I began to study biblical laments and found solace that I was not alone in my struggle. God placed an entire book, Lamentations, dedicated to laments in His word as a guide for how we can share our struggles with Him. Faithful men of God such as Jeremiah, David, and Job all struggled with depression and lamented to God. They found their hope in God and so would I. As Jeremiah wrote in Lamentations, God's love is endless and could never run out on me or others like me. I am learning to stick with God; He is truly all I have left. I wrestled with God and He wrestled for me. Even as I struggled, He never let me go.

REFLECTION & APPLICATION

1. Is there a time that you felt like you hit rock bottom?

2. There are many stories in the Bible describing bouts with depression and anxiety (David, Jonah, Job, Elijah). What do these experiences teach us and why?

3. Read Psalm 40:1-3 and reflect on how David dealt with a rock-bottom moment.

4. Grief and emotional pain are a normal experience. Learn how to take your pain to God and let His truth speak into your life. Stop and pray. Tell God your unfiltered, unedited feelings. Then listen.

Father, we praise You that though we wrestle, You never let us go. Thank You for the people of the Bible who remind us of the struggles and pain of living in this world and give voice to our laments. Though we taste the ash and the poison, may You be our hope and our salvation.

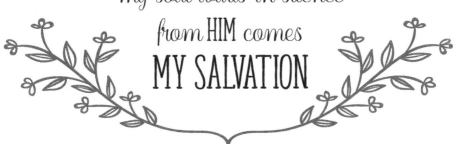

for GOD alone
my soul waits in silence
from HIM comes
MY SALVATION

PSALM 62:1

BLESSINGS

LAURA STORY

We pray for blessings
We pray for peace
Comfort for family, protection while we sleep
We pray for healing, for prosperity
We pray for Your mighty hand to ease our suffering
All the while, You hear each spoken need
Yet love is way too much to give us lesser things

'Cause what if your blessings come through raindrops
What if Your healing comes through tears
What if a thousand sleepless nights are what it takes to know You're near
What if trials of this life are Your mercies in disguise

We pray for wisdom, your voice to hear
We cry in anger when we cannot feel You near
We doubt your goodness, we doubt your love
As if every promise from Your Word is not enough
All the while, You hear each desperate plea
And long that we'd have faith to believe

'Cause what if your blessings come through raindrops
What if Your healing comes through tears
What if a thousand sleepless nights are what it takes to know You're near
What if trials of this life are Your mercies in disguise

When friends betray us
When darkness seems to win
We know that pain reminds this heart
That this is not our home

What if my greatest disappointments
Or the aching of this life
Is the revealing of a greater thirst this world can't satisfy
What if trials of this life
The rain, the storms, the hardest nights
Are your mercies in disguise

QUIET WAITING (PART 2)

REENA MCCORMICK

"God proves to be good to the man who passionately waits, to the woman who diligently seeks. It's a good thing to quietly hope, quietly hope for help from God. It's a good thing when you're young to stick it out through the hard times. When life is heavy and hard to take, go off by yourself. Enter the silence. Bow in prayer. Don't ask questions: Wait for hope to appear. Don't run from trouble. Take it full-face. The "worst" is never the worst."

"Why? Because the Master won't ever walk out and fail to return. If he works severely, he also works tenderly. His stockpiles of loyal love are immense. He takes no pleasure in making life hard, in throwing roadblocks in the way."

Lamentations 3:25-33 *The Message*

Sometimes things get worse before they get better. As doctors tried to figure out my medications, weekly prescription changes affected every part of me: physically, mentally, spiritually, and emotionally. Then I began to struggle with intense pain in my neck, weakness and nerve damage down my right arm, and migraines. A false diagnosis of fibromyalgia led to more medications, and these changes came with side effects like suicidal ideation and the inability to regulate my emotions. I felt battered on every side.

At the same time, I continued with the intensive outpatient therapy and it hurt. I had deep pain from wounds in our marriage I had not worked through, released, and forgiven. As these came to light, I wanted nothing more than to hide under the covers and wish it all away! As I surrendered daily and prayed for new mercies, however, God began to teach me the importance of being in His presence.

Reena, you need to go off by yourself, wait silently before Me, and seek My face.

Yes, Lord, but there are the kids and the house and . . .

As a mom of girls ages eight, four, and two, I know the struggle of having to prioritize everyone else's needs above my own. What I discovered was that I couldn't afford not to make time for God. I was desperate. I needed to wait quietly in His presence and hope for His help. As with the writer of Lamentations, it was in these times of quiet waiting that God began to do His healing work in my life.

I remember a time during my struggle when a friend offered to watch my girls for a few hours so I could get some things done around the house. Instead, I did what the Lamentations recommended. I drove to a nearby park and walked into a wooded area. There I put some worship music on and I expressed to God my sorrow, frustration, despair, and confusion. I remember thinking, *God, I don't even know if You are real any more because I can't see You and I can't rationalize an invisible God.* It was not my finest moment, but it was a moment when I stood there, lamenting to the Lord in raw honesty and doubt. I waited as Lamentations suggested, and hope did indeed appear—in the way that only God can somehow work it out.

When I left that time with God, I knew without a shadow of a doubt that He would bring my healing. I didn't know how long I would struggle with the depression, but I knew God was real and my healing would come only from him.

And these times of quiet waiting—as difficult as they were to endure—were essential to the process.

REFLECTION & APPLICATION

1. Describe a time and place where you felt God's presence. Give all the details to make it a vivid memory.

2. Throughout the gospels, we see Jesus going off to a quiet place. When and why did Jesus do this? Why do you need to do this?

3. Read Mark 1:35. Jesus nurtured His relationship with the Father through dedicated prayer and quiet time. How do you nurture your relationship with God? How can you do what Jesus did?

4. Challenge yourself to practice moments of solitude in the presence of God every day. Create a ten-minute retreat. Find a quiet place and time where you can spend five minutes in prayer and five minutes quietly listening to God.

Father, may I know in times of quiet waiting that You are still working in me. May I seek time alone with You when the burdens of the day threaten to drown that out. I pray that I would remember Your faithfulness in the past as I face the trials of today.

THE RESURRECTED KING
IS RESURRECTING ME

RESURRECTING

ELEVATION WORSHIP

The head that once was crowned with thorns
Is crowned with glory now
The Savior knelt to wash our feet
Now at his feet we bow

The one who wore our sin and shame
Now robed in majesty
The radiance of perfect love
Now shines for all to see

Your name
Your name
Is victory
All praise
Will rise
To Christ our king

The fear that held us now gives way
To him who is our peace
His final breath upon the cross
Is now alive in me

By Your spirit I will rise
From the ashes of defeat
The resurrected king
Is resurrecting me

In Your name I come alive
To declare your victory
The resurrected king
Is resurrecting me

The tomb where soldiers watched in vain
Was borrowed for three days
His body there would not remain
Our God has robbed the grave

Your name
Your name
Is victory
All praise
Will rise
To Christ our king

By Your spirit I will rise
From the ashes of defeat
The resurrected king
Is resurrecting me

In your name I come alive
To declare Your victory
The resurrected king
Is resurrecting me

MY STORY ISN`T FINISHED YET (PART 3)

REENA MCCORMICK

But Jacob stayed behind by himself, and a man wrestled with him until daybreak. When the man saw that he couldn't get the best of Jacob as they wrestled, he deliberately threw Jacob's hip out of joint. The man said, "Let me go; it's daybreak." Jacob said, "I'm not letting you go 'til you bless me." The man said, "What's your name?" He answered, "Jacob." The man said, "But no longer. Your name is no longer Jacob. From now on it's Israel (God-Wrestler); you've wrestled with God and you've come through." Jacob asked, "And what's your name?" The man said, "Why do you want to know my name?" And then, right then and there, he blessed him. Jacob named the place Peniel (God's Face) because, he said, "I saw God face-to-face and lived to tell the story!"

Genesis 32:24-30

While I was hopeful the Lord was beginning to heal me emotionally and spiritually, my physical pain got worse. By God's grace, I was referred to a spine surgeon. He scheduled an MRI, which showed I had herniated discs at C3-C4 and C5-C6. This brought clarity to the pain but also the realization that I had been misdiagnosed with fibromyalgia and my medication would have to be switched yet again.

At this point, the psychiatrist apologized. He told me I had not been validated for most of my life and my opinion had been devalued when I was not part of the decision-making process for my medication changes. Together, we decided I would wean off some of the medications that were negatively affecting me. This process was full of hazards, for the side effects of withdrawal can make people think they need the medication to live. One part of me knew I needed to push through but another part worried as to whether I would survive or not. The withdrawal process was hell on earth.

This was one of the lowest times in my life. I remember getting into an argument with my husband one Sunday after church. He was so frustrated with me that he just let me leave by myself. I drove off to a parking lot, sat in my car, and cried. I had a friend from our Side By Side-Pittsburgh group to whom I often reached out when I wasn't doing well. I texted her and she asked if she could meet me, but it was Sunday. I figured she was with her family, and didn't want to bother her, but in hindsight I should have. I then drove to a park and tried to quiet my heart by journaling.

My husband called several times and though his intentions were good, it just escalated my emotions. As I sat in the car, I thought, "If I just hit the gas with all my strength, I can run into the building in front of me and everyone will be better off. My husband wouldn't have an unstable wife and my kids wouldn't grow up with a mother who was traumatizing them. It would fix everything and everyone would be better off." My husband reached out to my father who begged me to come home. It's only by God's grace that I was able to calm down and drive home.

A few weeks later on Easter Sunday, a friend encouraged me to ask for prayer at church. I asked for prayer regarding migraines and neck pain, but explained my real pain came from my battle with depression. Two pastors anointed my head with oil and prayed for me. They encouraged me to examine my heart for the source of my pain. I began to confess the roots of my depression, which was caused by unforgiveness and jealousy. As I cried out to God for forgiveness, God began to work through these pastors as He gave them words to speak that only I could understand.

I knew my depression came from years of putting myself down for not being smart enough, good enough, and worthy enough of God's love. As the pastors prayed, however, God revealed that I started to believe those lies when I was held back in second grade and bullied by other kids. It was such a painful time that I had blocked it out. Once I understood the root of these lies, I was able to surrender. I felt freedom and, for the first time in a long time, I believed God loved me. I felt the weight of fourteen years of depression lift off me. God had given me hope and strength to continue this journey. Like Jacob, I had wrestled with my reality and found relief and victory over my old ways of thinking and acting.

As a bookend to this season of suffering, I decided to undergo surgery to remove the herniated disc at C3-C4 and fuse my vertebrae at that spot after lots of physical therapy and medical considerations. It has been a painful recovery and I have a surgical scar on the front of my neck, but I am hopeful. Just as God gave Jacob a limp when he wrestled with God, I wear a scar on my neck as a daily reminder of all He has brought me through—physically, mentally, spiritually and emotionally—and of His steadfast faithfulness to me.

I was later able to join a research study that looked at my cerebrospinal fluid and genetic testing that indicated my body does not create adequate serotonin or dopamine. This confirmed that the medications I had been on for 14 years were not helping and most likely making things worse. I continue to work with doctors who have helped me find the best treatment plan for my body.

God doesn't always answer our prayers the way we hope. Sometimes the miracles we ask for don't come and we go through seasons of pain, grief, and suffering. In the moments when it's too heavy to bear and we feel like we are suffocating, it's important to remember: God was faithful before and He will continue to be faithful again and again.

One of God's greatest mercies is when we live through something we thought would destroy us and come out the other side. We may emerge with scars and bruises, but also with new strength and a renewed faith. This experience has taught me many things, but most importantly it has taught me to seek the face of Jesus, to desire Him in a new and intimate way, to wait patiently on Him, and to trust that He is faithful.

Because of Jesus, my story is not finished yet.

REFLECTION & APPLICATION

1. Your testimony is the point where the gospel collides with the reality of your life. Make a list of characteristics that describe you before you came to Jesus and then a second list that describes how God has changed you.

2. The Bible is full of stories about broken heroes who had struggles in their lives, but their stories include how God redeemed and used them for His good purposes. Who is your favorite broken hero and why? What lessons can you glean from that hero's life that you can apply to your own?

3. Read Acts 26:1-29. Paul gave his testimony to King Agrippa while he was on trial for his life. Do you ever feel uncomfortable sharing how God has changed your life? Someone once said that your best testimony is the one you don't want to share. Which part of your testimony makes you uncomfortable?

4. Like Jacob becoming Israel, God has given you a new identity and is changing you into a new person. Where are you wrestling with God as Jacob did? What is your testimony that resulted from that struggle? Is that struggle ongoing or can you see that you are a changed person, even if you walk with a limp?

Father, thank You that when the weight of this life presses in all our sides, I am not crushed. May I seek Your face daily, wait patiently on You, and remember Your past faithfulness. Lord, I know that even these disciplines begin with repentance and reliance on You. My hope rests in You!

Reena McCormick was born and raised in Pittsburgh and has been hosting the Side By Side-Pittsburgh evening group for ten years. She and Andy met in biology class at Grove City College and have been married for 14 years. Reena is a pediatric occupational therapist at the Children's Hospital where her husband also works as a hospitalist. Their three daughters, Arathena, Asha, and Daya, love hosting Side By Side as much as their mother. Reena's mother, Molly, battled Alzheimer's for 16 years and played a major role in their lives. She passed away right before this book was published.

He has made everything beautiful in its time

ECCLESIASTES 3:11

THE PERFECT WISDOM OF OUR GOD

STUART TOWNEND AND KEITH GETTY

The perfect wisdom of our God,
Revealed in all the universe:
All things created by His hand,
And held together at His command.
He knows the mysteries of the seas,
The secrets of the stars are His;
He guides the planets on their way,
And turns the earth through another day.

The matchless wisdom of His ways,
That mark the path of righteousness;
His word a lamp unto my feet,
His Spirit teaching and guiding me.
And oh, the mystery of the cross,
That God should suffer for the lost
So that the fool might shame the wise,
And all the glory might go to Christ!

Oh grant me wisdom from above,
To pray for peace and cling to love,
And teach me humbly to receive
The sun and rain of Your sovereignty.
Each strand of sorrow has a place
Within this tapestry of grace;
So through the trials I choose to say:
"Your perfect will in your perfect way."

LIFE IS A TAPESTRY

SARAH CUDNEY

My Life is but a weaving
between my Lord and me;
I cannot choose the colors
He worketh steadily.
Oft times He weaveth sorrow
And I, in foolish pride,
Forget He sees the upper,
And I the underside.
Not till the loom is silent
And the shuttles cease to fly,
Shall God unroll the canvas
And explain the reason why.
The dark threads are as needful
In the Weaver's skillful hand,
As the threads of gold and silver
In the pattern He has planned.

Author Unknown

My life is similar to a tapestry, and I can only see the back. This analogy resonates with me, especially when my life appears to be nothing more than a jumble of thread—tangled, frayed, knotted, and seemingly random. Nothing makes sense, and yet a beautiful tapestry is being woven.

In my life, there has been a lot of joy—gold threads in my tapestry. I have three beautiful boys, a physician husband who loves me and provides for our family, and good friends. At the same time, there has also been a lot of pain.

In 2008, my 26-year-old brother took his life. He was tall and handsome, a graduate of Northwestern University with a degree in mechanical engineering, and a talented artist. I do not understand why he purposely ended his life—he left no note—and the guilt I still have over not doing something to help him is immense. The year after his death was unbearably difficult. My husband was working long hours in his residency and could offer little support as I grieved. I had a demanding teaching job and did not have the support I needed to help me through the darkness. In my tapestry, the threads from this time are quite dark.

Grief slowly gave way to healing as I joined my local Side By Side group and built close friendships. With immense joy, my husband and I welcomed children into the world—more gold threads. Then, when my second son was six months old, he was hospitalized with a virus and was diagnosed "failure to thrive." He spent 28 days in the hospital and could only be fed through an intravenous tube because his intestines lost the ability to absorb any nutrients. Again, I did not understand why dark threads were being woven into my tapestry. I spent many tearful days agonizing over why he would not get better. My Side By Side group stood by me during this time by bringing me meals, staying with my son in the hospital so I could run home to shower, and praying with me. God showed me His faithfulness through these women.

That was the start of a long series of doctor visits. We discovered that he has a lifelong digestive disorder that we are now able to treat with medication and, for the most part, he lives a normal life. Again, dark threads have given way to golden ones, as my son has brought us so much joy and leads a (mostly) healthy life.

Proverbs 19:21 says, "Many are the plans in a person's heart, but it is the Lord's purpose that prevails" (NIV). If I get caught up seeing the underside of my tapestry, I may not see the beautiful purpose that God has for both the gold and dark threads. I might forget that a tapestry of all gold threads would not be interesting at all. The final verse of a hymn I recently sang in church brought me to tears as I thought about God weaving the threads of my life:

The Perfect Wisdom of Our God
by Stuart Townend and Keith Getty
O grant me wisdom from above,
To pray for peace and cling to love,
And teach me humbly to receive
The sun and rain of Your sovereignty.
Each strand of sorrow has a place
Within this tapestry of grace;
So through the trials I choose to say:
"Your perfect will in Your perfect way."

My prayer is that you will know that God has a beautiful purpose for you. Your life is a tapestry that He is weaving according to His perfect will.

REFLECTION & APPLICATION
1. What are some gold threads in your tapestry? What are your dark threads?

2. What key verses, prayers, songs, or books get you through your dark-thread times? What is helpful or comforting to you about them?

3. Ecclesiastes 3:11 says "He has made everything beautiful in its time." Is there an ugly situation in your life that you need to surrender to God? How has God already "made everything beautiful in its time" in your life?

Father, I thank You for the story You are writing in my life. As I look at the dark threads of trial and pain, help me lean on You for peace and understanding. Help me see Your loving plan for my life and trust You as the author of my faith.

Sarah Cudney and her husband, Nick, live outside of Chicago, IL. Sarah was involved in Side By Side-Pittsburgh from 2009 to 2013 while her husband completed his oral and maxillofacial surgery residency in Pittsburgh. Sarah taught high school science until having children, and she now stays home with their three boys and works part-time as a photographer.

63

And my God will
supply every need
of yours according to his riches in
glory in Christ Jesus

TRUST IN YOU

LAUREN DAIGLE

Letting go of every single dream
I lay each one down at Your feet
Every moment of my wandering
Never changes what You see

I try to win this war
I confess, my hands are weary, I need Your rest
Mighty warrior, king of the fight
No matter what I face You're by my side

When You don't move the mountains
I'm needing You to move
When You don't part the waters
I wish I could walk through
When You don't give the answers
As I cry out to You
I will trust, I will trust, I will trust in You

Truth is, You know what tomorrow brings
There's not a day ahead You have not seen
So let all things be my life and breath
I want what You want Lord and nothing less

You are my strength and comfort
You are my steady hand
You are my firm foundation
The rock on which I stand
Your ways are always higher
Your plans are always good
There's not a place where I'll go
You've not already stood

When You don't move the mountains
I'm needing You to move
When You don't part the waters
I wish I could walk through
When You don't give the answers
As I cry out to You
I will trust, I will trust, I will trust in You

REFINER'S FIRE

LAUREN RUTKOSKI

"So that the tested genuineness of your faith—more precious than gold that perishes though it is tested by fire—may be found to result in praise and glory and honor at the revelation of Jesus."

1 Peter 1:7

Looking back at our early dating years, one of the things that attracted me to my husband was the allure of his career as a physician. I'm not proud to admit such a seemingly shallow attraction, though I did desperately crave stability (and perhaps a bit of prestige). At face value, these seem rather benign desires. God in His grace revealed to me over the course of oh-so-many upsets that those desires grew from malignant and defective roots, which eventually produced rotten fruit.

When we left Pittsburgh to New Jersey for my husband's fellowship, we didn't anticipate a return to our beloved city. When a position at a small community hospital just west of Pittsburgh opened up, however, we were more than thrilled. Some remarkable connections of my friend's husband's brother's father-in-law-to-be landed my husband the job, and our family came to a town rivaling Mayberry with its tight-knit charm.

After much adieu (living for a month in my husband's parent's home, one month in his sister's home, and finally one more month in the home of his future partner), we finally found and settled into my dream home. We were warmly welcomed into the community and, quite frankly, tasted just a hint of celebrity status—my husband's handsome face graced a giant, impossible-to-miss billboard on the bridge into town. Indeed, after much toil, training, transition, hoping, and praying, we had "arrived."

While we started to settle into that comfort I had always wanted, I was distraught to realize there was still chaos roaring in my heart. I was anxious, bored, and my head was spinning. I desperately struggled to quiet it all. If I could just get my house "just so," if I could better discipline my time, if I could live up to this perceived identity as a respected physician's wife who has it all together, if, if, if.

Alas, I was never allowed the opportunity to "get it together." After only six months, my husband was informed by the partners in his practice that things were not working out. We'd both recognized that the learning curve with a first job is a sharp one, and my husband's start had not been the smoothest, but even so, to say we were shocked would be an understatement. How swift a fall from glory!

My high-achieving, hard-working, rarely-rattled husband was baffled. Our emotions ran the gamut from disbelief *(How could this happen? You're such an easy-going guy, how could there possibly be conflict?)* to anger *(How dare they not extend more grace? Where was the constructive feedback, the mentoring?)* to shame and fear *(Is this even what you're supposed to be doing? Have we missed the boat entirely?)*. Suddenly there was no job, no salary, no back-up plan, and we had not one, but two mortgages—three if you count medical school loans. Hadn't God led us here? Hadn't He opened some heavy doors and provided blossoming friendships, a lively community, and a loving church family? He couldn't possibly have something different in store. What more could there be?

God, in His goodness, answered this question with "immeasurably more than we could ask or imagine" (Ephesians 3:20). Amidst all these raw emotions and tangible needs, God provided abundantly. At the same time, He gently showed me how He loved me far too much to allow feeble substitutes for Him to reign in my heart. I had mistakenly placed my hope and trust in my husband's job, his skills, his training, and his ability to provide. These good gifts had become idols, taking the place of God's rightful throne in my heart. Until they were shaken, I had no idea how faulty my foundation of faith was. God used these experiences to refine me as Peter wrote in 1 Peter 1:7.

As terrifying an experience as it was at the time, it revealed some hard-to-face truths—truths that had long lived in my head but had not made the journey to my heart. So little of what we were experiencing made sense, but God showed me that many times we are allowed only glimpses of the much bigger picture He has planned. His ways are not our ways, His thoughts are not our thoughts (see Isaiah 55:8).

Now, after some major uprooting, a lot of tears, and many prayers, the Lord has led us to a new city, new friends, and a new church community. My husband is working in a new specialty which, by God's grace, allows more family and free time than we could ever have hoped. And I am learning new lessons daily, grounded by a more authentic grasp of truth. I have learned to hold any notion of *mine, safety,* or *forever* much more loosely than before. With my grip relaxed, I am better able to offer my time, heart, and resources to others. All I have is His and all He has is mine. This is—and I pray always will be—more than enough.

REFLECTION & APPLICATION

1. Can you think of a time in your life when plans completely changed or big expectations were disappointed? How did you respond?

2. Read Exodus 34:6-7 where God describes His own character to Moses. Spend time meditating on this passage. What are the qualities of God's character in these verses?

3. Read Exodus 20:3-5. An idol is anything we put before the Lord (thus giving it more of our time, our energy, our affections). Are there good gifts in your life that have become idols (consider money, family, affirmation, comfort, physical appearance, control)?

4. What steps could you take to surrender these to the Lord?

Father, help me to hold loosely to any notions of mine, safety, and forever. May all that I have in You be enough. Keep me from idolizing the things of this world and set my heart to worshiping You instead.

Lauren Rutkoski originally connected with Side By Side-Pittsburgh during her husband John's surgical residency. After four treasured years of involvement, they ultimately landed in Buffalo, NY, where they currently reside with their two children. Lauren works part-time as a physician's assistant and is grateful to be involved with her local Side By Side chapter.

i can do
ALL THINGS

through

CHRIST

who STRENGTHENS ME

PHILIPPIANS 4:13

MY STORY

BIG DADDY WEAVE

If I told you my story
You would hear Hope that wouldn't let go
And if I told you my story
You would hear Love that never gave up
And if I told you my story
You would hear Life, but it wasn't mine

If I should speak then let it be
Of the grace that is greater than all my sin
Of when justice was served and where mercy wins
Of the kindness of Jesus that draws me in
Oh to tell you my story is to tell of Him

If I told you my story
You would hear victory over the enemy
And if I told you my story
You would hear freedom that was won for me
And if I told you my story
You would hear Life overcome the grave

If I should speak then let it be
Of the grace that is greater than all my sin
Of when justice was served and where mercy wins
Of the kindness of Jesus that draws me in
Oh to tell you my story is to tell of Him

This is my story, this is my song, Praising my savior all the day long
This is my story, this is my song, Praising my savior all the day long

PROVISION AND PROMISES

SARAH LAUDERMILCH

"And the Lord, He is the One who goes before you. He will be with you, He will not leave you nor forsake you; do not fear nor be dismayed."

Deuteronomy 31:8 NKJV

As I sit down to write this devotional, my house is quiet. My children are asleep and my husband is away on his first temporary duty assignment (TDY). A TDY means that he is assigned to another base or duty for a period of time that takes him away from his permanently-stationed base, home, and family. He was informed of the exact date of his TDY four days before he departed with a one-way ticket. As I write, he is on his way to another country as part of a medical team to aid the President of the United States while he is traveling overseas.

This TDY is just one example of how practicing medicine in the military fills me with pride, forces me to be extremely flexible, and allows my faith to be strengthened.

Pride is satisfaction derived from one's own achievements or those of whom one is closely associated. We have been an active part of the United States Air Force now for a full year. As we watch fighter jets practicing daily, paratroopers jumping out of planes, and ground forces marching with fully-loaded packs, it gives us a great sense of pride in the men and women who are training to protect this country. My husband's job is to treat the soldiers' orthopaedic issues so they can perform their jobs. I am proud of my husband's contribution to the strength of our military.

Pride, however, does not override the challenges of his position. When I am given four days to prepare for an overseas deployment, I have a choice. I can be upset or extremely flexible. I choose to be flexible even though it is difficult to have him be away. Sometimes he misses holidays and events like the first day of school but thankfully, God has been preparing me for this over the last fifteen years.

My husband and I attended high school together, but then went to college four hours apart. Once we were married and he began medical school, there were long shifts at the hospital and weeks away training at a military hospital. Then residency began, making all the previous experiences seem easy.

With a surgical residency, there were extremely long shifts with only a few hours in between for him to come home to sleep, higher levels of stress, and few days off. During his first year of residency, I witnessed my husband's personality change. He struggled with depression as he processed the life-and-death decisions he was part of daily and the loss of time for any previous hobbies.

During his second year of residency, his work hours were at their longest and we were expecting our second child. I called him at the hospital to let him know I was probably in labor. It was Thanksgiving weekend and there was only one other resident in town to cover their service. The co-resident came to cover his shift and we delivered our baby, but within twenty-four hours he was back at the hospital to work the next shift and I was adjusting to being a mother of two and begging my doctor to discharge me on the day my husband would be available to drive me home. At the same time, I had left a teaching job, co-workers, and my normal routine to stay home and raise our children. Through all of these challenges, God was preparing me for this TDY and future deployments. I am so thankful for His provision and preparation.

God's provision through medical training and preparation for the future have strengthened my faith. Nine years ago, a co-worker and close friend asked me how I was going to handle a military life. My answer then and now is that God would be with me. God has proven repeatedly that He will not leave me. I can handle the long deployments and short-notice trips with faith in His promises.

When I do have times of despair, loneliness, and fear, I can remember the past provisions and His promises to go before me and be with me always.

REFLECTION & APPLICATION

1. Write about a time when circumstances quickly became out of your control. What was your attitude when you approached this situation?

2. When you are preparing mentally for a challenge ahead, what verses do you think of to give you strength?

3. Read Philippians 3:7-11. How can our trials in this life prepare us for our eternal life?

4. Are you facing a time of change and uncertainty? List tangible ways you can remain positive, flexible, and committed to prayer during this time.

Father, thank You for Your provision for each new day. Help me to remember Your faithfulness in the past and the eternal promises found in Your word. Ground my feet on these truths as I face the challenges before me today.

Sarah Laudermilch grew up on a dairy farm in Pennsylvania and married Dann, her high school sweetheart. She was involved in Side By Side-Pittsburgh from 2009 to 2015 while Dann completed medical school and an orthopaedic surgical residency. Sarah taught elementary school special education until staying home to raise their four children. They currently are serving with the United States Air Force in Alaska.

The Lord is MY STRENGTH and my song, and He has become MY SALVATION

EXODUS 15:2

HOW GREAT THOU ART

STUART K HINE

O Lord my God, when I in awesome wonder,
Consider all the worlds Thy hands have made;
I see the stars, I hear the rolling thunder,
Thy power throughout the universe displayed.

Then sings my soul, my Savior God, to Thee,
How great Thou art! How great Thou art!

When through the woods, and forest glades I wander,
And hear the birds sing sweetly in the trees.
When I look down, from lofty mountain grandeur
And hear the brook, and feel the gentle breeze.

And when I think, that God, His Son not sparing;
Sent Him to die, I scarce can take it in;
That on the cross, my burden gladly bearing,
He bled and died to take away my sin.

When Christ shall come, with shout of acclamation,
And take me home, what joy shall fill my heart.
Then shall I bow, in humble adoration,
And then proclaim, "My God, how great Thou art!"

Then sings my soul, my Savior God, to Thee,
How great Thou art! How great Thou art!

I DESERVE THAT

KRISTEN CHOBY

"When pride comes, then comes disgrace, but with the humble is wisdom."

Proverbs 11:2

On a beautiful Pennsylvania night, I sat on a swing with my wonderful husband-to-be. We sat and talked, a short but serious discussion about this life we were about to begin. "It's going to be hard," my fiancé kept repeating. I nodded, but inside I was thinking, "Sure, hard. Okay, I can handle hard. Isn't any marriage hard at first?" I had no idea what we were getting into!

After the wedding and honeymoon, medical school started back up and we embarked on "hard." The hours apart got longer and longer. I worked two jobs trying to stash up savings in case we had a baby at some point and all the while, loans were beginning to pile high. I was lonely, dealing with jealousy, not happy with my work situation, and stressed about finances. Worst of all, I felt like I was going at it all on my own.

In my husband's final year of medical school, he interviewed, at our expense, at nearly twenty different residency programs. There was pressure to find a good fit, as we were due the week of Match Day with our first child. Thankfully and through the grace of God, Match Day worked out well, and we were headed "home" to Pittsburgh, PA.

Though landing back in Pittsburgh was a huge blessing and I had much to be grateful for, I found myself and my marriage at a low point. Once our son was born, we decided that I would stay at home rather than pay for childcare. After interviewing, moving, and living without income for two months, our savings were gone. Though it's ridiculous to have "savings" with debt quickly accumulating, I had found comfort in that stash of cash, and suddenly it wasn't there.

Intern year was a complete whirlwind to us emotionally, physically and financially. The demands placed on my husband, our family, and marriage were huge. To top it off, we were pregnant with our second child. My husband's second year of residency was even more demanding, if that was possible. This is when my attitude hit a low point. We had been through a lot. Didn't we deserve better than this?

I know I certainly deserved to get a babysitter at least once a month. I deserved a break, sleep, better clothes, and maybe even a gym membership. We deserved to travel, nothing fancy, but just a small vacation, for sure. I deserved a husband, car, and apartment I could rely on, not an absentee husband and continually breaking-down stuff. My husband was working "79.5" hours a week, and we certainly did *not* deserve to be struggling financially. Most of all, I deserved love, happiness, and respect from my husband, for after all, it was for *his* career for which I had sacrificed so much. Yes, that's what I deserved. I know it's a long list, but how could it be too much to ask for a "normal" life?

After many fights and continued discouragement, my husband and I didn't even celebrate our anniversary that year. I said, "There's nothing to celebrate and we didn't have the money anyway." At that moment, it was clear that something had to change on the inside of me.

The world tells us that our marriages are supposed to be sexy and full of romance, with sparks, cuddling, and a soul mate who is everything we need him to be when we need it. The world says that as doctors' wives we are glamourous, without a care, and certainly not concerned about money.

God says the exact opposite of what the world says. He informs us that it is going to be difficult, but that we can come to completely rely on Him. We can rest in His word. He will provide all that we need.

Self-righteousness, anxiety, pride, hurt, blame, and anger were not the answer for my problems. Me, myself and I, the unholy trinity, needed to be replaced with something that was meant to be there.

Mercifully, God got a hold of me and started working on my heart. I got more involved in Side By Side where we were studying *The Power of a Praying Wife* by Stormie Omartian. I also started going to Christian counseling on my own. Through these things and the encouragement of godly women, God worked in me. Ultimately, all this trickled down into my marriage, relieving my anxiety and changing my attitude about "what I deserved."

God was the only one who could correctly fill a hole of pride as big as the one I had. Once I dove into Scripture and immersed myself in a good community, He provided the counsel, friendship, relief from financial anxiety, and adjustment in my thinking that only He could. "It's going to be hard," my husband had once said, but we had no idea how hard it could be. With my pride continually being chipped away, I am more open to the ways in which God will bring us through.

REFLECTION & APPLICATION

1. What are some things that you feel you "deserve"?

2. The world tells us we deserve much but Proverbs 16:18-19 states, "Pride goes before destruction, a haughty spirit before a fall. Better to be lowly in spirit along with the oppressed than to share plunder with the proud." What speaks to you in these verses?

3. Write a prayer of repentance for the pride in your life, asking God to work in you if these expectations are causing disturbances in you relationships and marriage. Ask God to reveal areas of pride you do not recognize or acknowledge.

Father, I thank You that You are not absent in the hard things of life. I pray that You would free me from prideful expectations of comfort and ease in this life, and instead open my eyes to the ways that You are working to make me more Christ-like through these trials. Help me to find support and strength through Scripture and the community of other believers.

MY HELP COMES FROM

the Lord

THE MAKER OF HEAVEN AND EARTH

PSALM 121:2 (NIV)

MY WORTH IS NOT IN WHAT I OWN

KEITH AND KRISTYN GETTY

My worth is not in what I own
Not in the strength of flesh and bone
But in the costly wounds of love
At the cross

My worth is not in skill or name
In win or lose, in pride or shame
But in the blood of Christ that flowed
At the cross

I rejoice in my Redeemer
Greatest Treasure, Wellspring of my soul
I will trust in Him, no other.
My soul is satisfied in Him alone.

As summer flowers we fade and die
Fame, youth and beauty hurry by, But life eternal calls to us
At the cross

I will not boast in wealth or might
Or human wisdom's fleeting light
But I will boast in knowing Christ
At the cross

Two wonders here that I confess
My worth and my unworthiness
My value fixed - my ransom paid
At the cross

PROVIDENCE

KRISTEN CHOBY

"So do not worry, saying, 'What shall we eat?' or 'What shall we drink?' or 'What shall we wear?' For the pagans run after all these things, and your heavenly Father knows that you need them."

Matthew 6:31-32

While many in our society equate being a physician with being wealthy, the initial financial investment in medical school can take years to regain. Even though our residency program did pay a reasonable salary, the burden of student loan debt repayments and a single-worker income was significant.

We were at a point financially where we could never get ahead. Walking into Walmart on a basic grocery trip would give me anxiety attacks. Even though I prepared an organized shopping list, I was overwhelmed by the aisles of stuff. I was frugal, but the constant comparing and price-checking was exhausting and after every trip, I walked out the door feeling despair about how much I was spending.

This theme of despair crossed over into every aspect of my life that involved spending money. An extra gift one month for a relative's birthday or even our monthly rent payment always brought on severe distress. It eventually became clear to me, however, that the fundamental issue was not the things on which I was spending our money but that I was not trusting God to take care of it all. I was counting on money to rescue me, but God had something else in mind.

As I loosened my grip on our finances, I became aware of God's financial blessings through many opportunities to support our family with part-time work and cost-saving living arrangements. I was able to provide babysitting and truly believe that God connected me with the little ones in my care and the families I helped. The love, prayer, laughs, and support in parenting that was formulated through these relationships are priceless to me.

Timely cleaning jobs would open up just when we had to cover an unplanned expense or to help us get a stroller. A family member surprised us and paid our rent one month. I even had the opportunity to indulge in my baking hobby and get paid to do so by a restaurant owned by a neighbor. And finally, as a final show of liberation from financial stress, we made a tough decision to move in with friends from church to help cut our rental costs drastically. In this situation, God provided the specific things we had prayed about that we believed would make cohabitation with friends work out well.

Each one of these opportunities came with its own lessons to be learned, and I have no doubt that God had pre-arranged them all. Yes, God provided for our physical needs and taught me not to stress about finances. He is so faithful and took things further than my selfish flesh could imagine. He allows me to have daily peace and contentment.

Of course, financial peace is not complete without feeling the freedom to give freely. God has used tithing to teach me about letting go of my anxiety about finances and is working in me to become a good and faithful steward. God uses tithing not for His benefit but for ours. Once we take that step of obedience and acknowledge that everything we have is from the Lord, He faithfully provides and teaches us to rely on him. Knowing that we are following God's word has been a huge source of contentment and relief. God has been so faithful in providing just what we need and helping me to lessen the stressors that come when dealing with finances. In this world of abundance and glittery stuff, His grace of contentment is the only attitude that truly works.

I thank God for providing more than I can ever see here on earth.

REFLECTION & APPLICATION

1. How has God provided for you? List the ways He has done so.

2. Read Psalm 121. What about this psalm comforts you concerning God's ability to provide?

3. Read Philippians 4:6-7. What does this passage teach you about how to deal with stress or anxiety?

4. Memorize Psalm 121 and Philippians 4:6-7. Pray and quote them in times of stress to remind your heart and mind that God is your good Provider.

Father, I thank You that You provide every single need that we have, not only financially, but in all other aspects of our life. I pray that You would free me from anxiety about finances or any need that presses me to be anxious and not to wait on You. Help me to trust in You and know that You will work all things for good.

Kristen Choby and her husband, Garret, began their walk down this medical life journey in 2008. Five moves, three boys and three states later, they finished a residency in otolaryngology and a fellowship in rhinology and endoscopic skull base surgery. Kristen was a member of Side By Side-Pittsburgh from 2012 to 2016. She currently works in her home raising their children in Rochester, Minnesota.

be KIND to one another,
TENDERHEARTED,
FORGIVING one another,
as God in Christ forgave you.

EPHESIANS 4:32

GOD BE MERCIFUL TO ME

JARS OF CLAY

God be merciful to me on Thy grace, I rest my plea
Plenteous in compassion Thou
Blot out my transgressions now

Wash me, make me pure within
Cleanse, oh, cleanse me from my sin

My transgressions I confess
Grief and guilt my soul oppress
I have sinned against Thy grace
And provoked Thee to Thy face

I confess Thy judgment just
Speechless, I, Thy mercy trust

I am evil born in sin
Thou desirest truth within
Thou alone my Savior art
Teach Thy wisdom to my heart

Make me pure, Thy grace bestow
Wash me whiter than the snow

Gracious God, my heart renew
Make my spirit right and true
Thy salvation's joy impart
Steadfast make my willing heart
Steadfast make my willing heart

Broken, humbled to the dust
By Thy wrath and judgment just
Let my contrite heart rejoice
And in gladness hear Thy voice

From my sins, oh, hide Thy face
Blot them out in boundless grace

FORGIVENESS (PART 1)

ASHLEY TALARICO

"Bear with each other and forgive whatever grievances you may have against one another. Forgive just as the Lord forgave you."

Colossians 3:13

I grew up in a wonderful Christian home and community. My parents were involved in our church where my dad taught the adult Sunday School class and my mom took on large projects like VBS and hospitality. Attendance at Sunday School and youth group was a part of our regular routine. By nature, I am a rule follower and was eager to follow the "rules" presented to us in youth group in order to be a good Christian.

"Forgive, as the Lord forgave you" was a rule I tried to follow, and I practiced forgiveness when a friend wronged me in some middle-school drama or a sibling stole my things. Then, when I was sixteen, my world shattered and this seemingly simple instruction took on a whole new depth.

One day out of nowhere, my mom awkwardly sat my siblings and me down and dropped a bomb: *Your dad and I are getting a divorce.* My dad then came in the room alone and told us he had been seeing another woman. He said he was sorry and that he still loved us. After this brief encounter, he walked out the door and our family was never intact again.

Adultery was not common in our community. It was shocking and confusing, and I felt angry and ashamed. We moved to a smaller house, visited my dad every other weekend, and watched my mom go through extreme heartache. For the first time in my life, I was put in a position of feeling deep hurt and anger from this injustice. I was angry at my dad and angry at God for allowing this to happen to my family.

At college, I found myself surrounded by like-minded Christians, and wrestled with questions about Christianity and God. This is when I started to see my own sin more clearly. James 4:4 says that we are an adulterous people in spirit when we abandon God for the world. This hit me at a deep level. I realized that just as my dad separated himself from our family, I too had separated myself from God and selfishly sought pleasures apart from him. Having experienced the pain of abandonment, it grieved me that I could make God feel this way.

For the first time, I felt I could forgive my dad. I wrote him a letter and expressed my forgiveness. I also expressed my desire for him to return to church and his relationship with the Lord. The letter was not received in the way I had hoped. He didn't ask for forgiveness and refused to repent. Still, I had taken a step toward forgiving him and God continued to lead me down quite a long road toward true forgiveness.

REFLECTION & APPLICATION

1. Think of a time when you struggled to forgive someone. What made it difficult to forgive them?

2. Read the parable of the unmerciful servant in Matthew 18:21-35. What does Jesus teach us about forgiveness?

3. Read Colossians 3:12-14. Paul encourages Christians to put to death their earthly ways and put on their new self in Christ. What one attribute did he say holds all the others together and what might it have to do with forgiveness?

4. Over the next week, pray that the Holy Spirit will reveal to you where in your life you are harboring unforgiveness. Pray that the Lord will guide you toward forgiveness and ask Him for forgiveness for your own sins.

Father, thank You for the complete forgiveness that I have through Your Son Jesus' death on the cross. I pray that I can repent of my own adulterous tendencies that cause me to love the things of this world more than You. As I understand the cost of my own salvation and depth of my sin, please help me to extend forgiveness to those who have wronged and hurt me.

··· *Mercy* ···

TRIUMPHS OVER

JUDGMENT

JAMES 2:13

MERCY

BETHEL MUSIC, AMANDA COOK

You delight in showing mercy
And mercy triumphs over judgement

My past embraced
My sin forgiven
I'm blameless in Your sight
My history rewritten

You delight in showing mercy
And mercy triumphs over judgement

Oh Love, great Love
Fear cannot be found in You
And there will never be a day
You're uncertain of the ones you choose

You delight in showing mercy
And mercy triumphs over judgement

I will awake
And spend my days
Loving the One who has raised me up
From death to life
From wrong to right
You're making all things beautiful

MERCY (PART 2)

"For judgment is without mercy to one who has shown no mercy. Mercy triumphs over judgment."

James 2:13

Bitterness has deep roots. Deep down, even though I felt I had forgiven my dad, I believed he still owed me. I expected extra gifts and lenient parenting boundaries in return for my pain and suffering. Anger would creep back in and was a recurring attitude of my heart toward my dad. I could easily feel a sense of "serves him right" delight when I saw him broken or struggling. My forgiveness was conditional, not true biblical forgiveness.

Fast forward a few years and I was twenty-nine and still single. I had learned marrying a Christian man did not guarantee lifelong faithfulness, but I still desired to be married, and I had many dear Christian friends marry before me. One of these close friends in particular was a special source of encouragement and wisdom about Christian marriage for me. Ironically, years later we both found ourselves in a lonely and spiritually desolate season of life. Over time, I watched my close friend, one of the most solid believers I knew, become involved in an emotional affair with another man. I heard the details, I saw how insidiously it began, and right before my eyes one of the dearest people to my heart again was having an extra-marital affair. Unlike my father, I watched my friend confess her affair to her husband, repent, and receive God's forgiveness. I saw her husband forgive her and fight fiercely for her sanctification. It truly was by God's grace that she became completely unbound and free of shame.

This was difficult for me to process and for a time I completely lost faith in marriage. I had been in a busy season where I was distant from God, living a selfish life, and influenced more by the world than God's truth. In spite of this, God pursued me and in a thousand beautiful ways showed me who He is. I had to stare my own sins in the face, name them, and repent. During this time, I studied David's life closely and came to know Psalm 51 by heart. In that psalm, David poured his heart out to God after committing adultery with Bathsheba. The gospel became richer and deeper to me. I grew in my relationship with the Lord. I came to hold fast to the truth that *only God's love is unfailing*. It was in my relationship with God where I found unwavering security in His love for me.

I had believed in my "good Sunday School girl" core that there were people who would commit sins and people who would commit *sins*. I was a sinner, not a *sinner*. What happened with my friend allowed me to see that none of us are immune from any *sin*. Through her experience, I saw that I could easily have been my friend and committed adultery, which made me realize I could do what my dad did to our family. Understanding I was a sinner, I no longer believed I was better than my dad. I no longer felt like he owed me. I found myself praying for him—for his salvation and that his relationship with the Lord to be restored. My heart moved away from judgment and toward love and mercy. I had finally forgiven my dad.

Also for the first time, I really understood the gospel. No longer was I negotiating with God, expecting good blessings in return for good behaviors. I was a broken sinner undeserving of God's grace. Previously, I had an unforgiving heart because I did not fully realize my own need for forgiveness. I could finally forgive, just as Christ had forgiven me.

Looking back, it's easy to see God's timing in this for my own marriage. It was shortly after this season that I started dating my husband. I was secure in God's love for me and at peace knowing my husband will fail me and I will fail him because we are sinners. The more we understand our sin and need for forgiveness, and the deeper we know God's great love for us and the extent He went to in order to reconcile us to Him, the deeper we can love and forgive one another.

REFLECTION & APPLICATION

1. Have you or any believer close to you ever committed a *sin*? How has this affected your view on life related to the sin? For example, has it altered your view of marriage, friendship, godly community, family, or finances, just to name a few.

2. How did forgiveness and repentance play a role in the situation from question 1?

3. Read the entire story of David, Uriah, Bathsheba, the prophet Nathan, and the children involved in 2 Samuel 11 and 12. How did David's sin affect each of these individuals?

4. Read Psalm 51. This was David's prayer of repentance to God. What strikes you as the key features of David's repentance? How will this affect your repentance when you sin or *sin*?

*Father, help me to see that I, like all others, am capable of **sin**. I pray that Your grace and forgiveness would become more beautiful to me as I seek to understand the weight of my sin that You bore on the cross. Thank You that we all come to You as broken sinners and I pray that even in our brokenness (and because of our brokenness), we can point others to the hope of forgiveness through the cross.*

Ashley Talarico and her husband, Justin, currently live in the Dallas/Fort Worth, TX area. She is a mom of three and family medicine physician, and became involved in Side By Side-Pittsburgh during her husband's emergency medicine residency in Pittsburgh from 2014 to 2017.

come to

ME

all you who are
weary and burdened, and

I

will give you rest

MATTHEW 11:28 (NIV)

FIND REST

DARA MACLEAN

Life was formed in Your hands
You alone tell my story
All my hours like sand
I surrender all

Through the battle I'll sing
Lord, I know You are for me
My whole heart I will bring
I surrender all

In You I find rest, I find rest, in You I find rest
In You I find rest, I find rest, in You I find rest

In my deepest of fears
In my hours of weakness
From an ocean of tears
I surrender all

For Your word is my sword
And Your arms are my fortress
I know victory is Yours
I surrender all

Though the darkness falls
And the storms are raging
I will find my shelter in You, in You
Fount of mercy new
God of love unchanging
Now my heart is resting in You

In You I find rest, I find rest, in You I find rest
In You I find rest, I find rest, in You I find rest

Life was formed in Your hand
You alone tell my story
All my hours like sand
I surrender all

I WILL GIVE YOU REST

TRINA WILLSON

Then he said to them, "The Sabbath was made for man,
not man for the Sabbath."

Mark 2:27

When my husband and I decided that he would take a difficult surgical residency, we had one toddler. When he finished, five years later, we had five kids under the age of six! The time of my husband's residency was one of the most exhausting and formative seasons of my life.

I gave birth just as his residency was beginning, knowing that things would be busy with two young children and that I would spend the next few years parenting as a "single mom." Imagine our surprise when we found the Lord leading us to foster and adopt during those same challenging years. I had long felt God's call to adopt, and had talked with my husband from the time we were dating about adopting some day. We always felt that our adoptions would happen later, yet God began to bring up foster care repeatedly during the second year of residency.

Then our church began a foster and adoption ministry, offering licensing classes at church on Sunday mornings. We knew it was the only way we could make it work during that busy season; the Lord was paving the way for us to move forward. Ultimately, we first fostered and then adopted a sibling set of two over the next two years. At the same time, we got pregnant and gave birth to our third biological child.

During this time, we were both burning the candle at both ends. My husband got up in the wee hours of the morning and worked until after the kids were in bed, typically not even seeing them during the weekdays. I cared for five very young children who were unable to dress themselves or put on their own shoes. We were both overworked and I, in particular, was depressed and angry. I felt that the road was too long to see a light at the end of the tunnel.

I told myself to buck up, do better, have more patience with my children, not feel neglected by my husband's hours (over which he had no control), but still I felt unhappy, impatient, and neglected. I was drowning and afraid to admit to myself, much less anyone else, that I was angry with God for leading us into such a difficult season in our lives, with everything happening simultaneously. I spent time praying that God would ease the difficult journey we were walking, but didn't feel any of it lifting, so I began to turn away. I stopped praying; He must not be listening.

The struggle went on for a couple of years. My husband encouraged me to hire help. He felt that I ought to get help with the kids in the afternoon, but I fought the financial burden of paying for a regular sitter. My husband said that it was worth making sacrifices financially for my sanity. Ultimately, we agreed to hire a mother's helper for the kids during dinner prep and we also decided to set a weekly date night.

When my husband was able, we would go on a date. Even if we had to make it really cheap or short, like a walk in a park, we would get some time to reconnect. We also decided that on nights when he couldn't make it home in time for date night, I would go out by myself. I would have time alone or with friends every single week. At first I felt guilty over the selfish luxury of spending money on babysitting. I quickly began to see changes in my mental and emotional health, however, and my anger toward God diminished. I realized that God hadn't been surprised by my exhaustion, but neither had my Abba Father been telling me to pull myself up by my own bootstraps and work harder.

God knew what I needed. After all, He had already completed a big job, even bigger than my child rearing. He created the light and dark; the sky; the earth and sea, the sun, moon, and stars; the animals, birds, and fish; and the people. Then He rested from his work on the seventh day.

How could I have believed that rest was a luxury?

After moving from residency to fellowship, my husband's hours improved, and I realized how vital our time together had been for our relationship. I also saw how time to myself had made me a better mother and wife. Now I see what God knew all along.

REFLECTION & APPLICATION

1. What does the Sabbath look like for you and why is this important to your week?

2. Read 1 Kings 19:3-8. Do you ever feel like Elijah (running well past exhaustion)? What makes you feel this way?

3. Read Exodus 20 8:11. Why do you think God gave us the example of rest on the seventh day and where can you find examples in the Bible to support your thoughts?

4. What are three ways that you could institute more Sabbath time in your weekly routine and set apart more time to dedicate to rest and worship?

Father, remind me that rest is not a luxury but a command (and gift) from You. I pray that I would not be tempted by the wisdom of this world to pull myself up by my bootstraps and dive head first into busyness. In times of rest, may I be refreshed and come to know You better.

Trina Willson is an audiologist and her husband, Tom, is an ENT in the Air Force. She is currently working as a research audiologist at the Hearing Center for Excellence at Lackland Air Force Base in San Antonio, Texas.

She and her husband have been married for twelve years and have five crazy kids. She joined Side By Side in Texas in the early years of her husband's residency and it helped her through those long years. Trina was part of Side By Side-Pittsburgh from 2015 until 2016.

for I know THE PLANS I have for you

JEREMIAH 29:11 (NIV)

FROM THE INSIDE OUT

HILLSONG

A thousand times I've failed
Still your mercy remains
Should I stumble again
Still I'm caught in your grace
Everlasting, your light will shine when all else fades
Never ending, your glory goes beyond all fame

Your will above all else
My purpose remains
The art of losing myself in bringing you praise
Everlasting, your light will shine when all else fades
Never ending, your glory goes beyond all fame

My heart and my soul
I give you control
Consume me from the inside out Lord
Let justice and praise
Become my embrace
To love you from the inside out

Everlasting, your light will shine when all else fades
Never ending, your glory goes beyond all fame
And the cry of my heart is to bring you praise
From the inside out
Lord my soul cries out

OPEN HANDS

RACHEL SCHREITER

"For I know the plans I have for you," declares the Lord, "plans to prosper you and not to harm you, plans to give you hope and a future."

Jeremiah 29:11

I recently attended a conference with my husband. On the way, I prayed that it would be a time where God would speak into our marriage and my identity, two areas in which I had been struggling for several years. Within twenty-four hours after we landed in San Diego, God did what I asked.

I'd been hanging out in a doubtful place for a while, focused on self-worth and my purpose, particularly as it related to my ten years as a special educator. Then my husband found out he would be going to Pittsburgh for his fellowship. When we moved, God physically shut the door to my full-time job. Though I had been struggling in my field and feeling led to some kind of change, this closed door felt out of "my timeline." I also hadn't realized how much of my identity was wrapped up in my work; right under all of this was pride—I didn't want to let go of myself so my husband could move forward.

It had been a season of great instability in my head and heart. It had been a season of trying to trust that resurrection and freedom were on their way, but finding trust for those things was difficult.

Being at the conference really softened my heart for my husband's work. I discovered that his work does interest me and that what he is doing is good and important. I needed that. I needed to be there and see his networks and lifestyle and recognize the possibility for connectivity and ministry. I had been caught up in the resentment that accompanies really long work hours that left me feeling apart from him.

God gave me the strength to finally let this all go during this trip and asked me to step closer to Him. I put to death the parts of my life that I thought would give me the energy, reinforcement, and attention I needed. Now I'm trying to look out with my hands open, paying attention to my need for God to be the energy behind what I do instead of my own weak strength. I'm experiencing more joy in being home with my children for the time being, taking small steps to new opportunities, and finally lifting my stubborn head up and out at all the possibilities that lie ahead.

I'm learning to trust that seasons come and they go. Ones that are good will grow roots to help sustain me when the hard ones come. Those hard ones will reveal developed branches to keep us moving up and onward. Sometimes we may even return to things of old in previous seasons with new eyes, new roots, and new branches to take in the grace that comes with redemption. While bits and pieces of this story feel confusing and uncomfortable, the whole story of all this is God's gracious role in my life. Living in the present and trusting God's sovereign plan for me is very freeing. I prayed for freedom and God gave me an identity in Him—a secure, open-handed, loving identity in Him. My pride, insecurity, selfishness, and everything else human will get in the way daily, but He is always there.

I'm aware of my limits as a mom and need to pray hourly for the ability to focus on God's greatest creations in my life while they are right in front of me. I'm also aware of these seeds He is planting to stir up possibilities that bring healing, creativity, and connectivity as well as celebrating and giving space for my husband to answer his call too.

Now I am taking classes to pursue a new path that has led to a greater relationship with Christ. I am seeing the purpose of God's revelations in my heart as they relate to community and the relationships we have on this Earth. Side By Side has been an invaluable community through which God has worked in my life, showing me His story in each of the family's lives and experiences. I see the Kingdom He is building, side by side with one another, to glorify His name as an audience of one.

REFLECTION & APPLICATION

1. Life is a journey of peaks and valleys. The valleys can be disorienting. Have you had a time when you felt like you had forgotten who you were?

2. Read John 13:36-38; 18:15-18; 18:25-27; and 21:15-19. Peter was in a valley after Jesus was arrested and he denied Jesus three times. In John 21:15-19, how does Jesus restore Peter?

3. Have you had a time when you needed God to restore you?

4. Write your story, or some part of it, and share it with a friend.

Father, help me unclench my fists and open my hands in surrender to You. You have always known what is best for me and Your perfect will is my desire. Help me find contentment in the here-and-now and continue to birth new dreams in my heart as I seek to walk with You.

Rachel Schreiter and her husband, Ryan, live outside Philadelphia, PA. Rachel is currently at home with their two children and pursuing a masters in biblical counseling. Ryan is a physician at Temple University, practicing non-operative sports medicine. Rachel was part of Side By Side-Pittsburgh from 2015 to 2016.

FINAL THOUGHTS

When I think of God's providence and how He orchestrates every detail of our lives, I am amazed that He positioned me to minister to women in medical marriages. I grew up in an Indian home where my parents dreamed of arranging my marriage to a nice doctor. In my mind, however, marrying a doctor was the last thing I wanted to do! To my surprise, I found myself in a medical marriage when my smart and handsome lab partner swept me off my feet in undergraduate school. Although this was not the path I desired or intended, it has brought me great joy in my life, which includes ministering through Side By Side-Pittsburgh and living life with the ladies featured in this book.

Each of these sisters has impacted my life in a tangible way. They have taught me the importance of community and vulnerability and through them, God has taught me to pray fervently, lament to Him on their behalf, and slowly release and surrender what I held on to with clenched fists. I am blessed to have had a front-row seat to watch how God has worked in each of their lives and answered prayers in miraculous ways, and I wanted their stories to be shared. For some, this was a difficult task when they were asked to expose raw emotions to strangers and relive painful memories. To their credit, they were obedient to the call and I hope you have been blessed by what they shared— I know I was.

I thank each of these ladies for taking the risk and stepping out in faith to share their stories. I love you all deeply with a love only God can supply. I want to especially thank Lindsey Boone for proofreading and securing licenses for the songs, Kristen Choby for giving direction to the devotional questions, Rachel Luenberger for writing the prayers at the end of each entry, and Sarah Cudney for finding a loom artist and taking the beautiful cover photo.

Thank you, Jen Pelling, for believing in our project and helping us edit and unify our original work. You did a remarkable job with such a difficult task.

Thank you, Shillika Chandrasekhar, for designing the cover and formatting the piece to make it beautiful. You always knew how to ease my fears and transform my mountains into gently rolling hills.

Thank you, Dr. John Stanko and Urban Press, for making this process seem effortless. It has been a joy to work with you.

Thank you, Robin Morgenthaler, for your vision to start Side By Side and Heidi Sems for your mentorship as our regional director.

Thanks to Andy, my husband, who believed in this project from its inception and has supported us every step of the way from proofreading and writing questions to watching kids so we could meet. I also want to thank my dear children who gave me the time and space I needed to finish this project. I witnessed the sacrifices you all made and I am grateful to you. I promise we will have a clean house again one day!

Since 2009, my family has opened our living room and our hearts to the women of Side By Side-Pittsburgh. It's a small space where we pile on top of each other and share life's struggles while encouraging each other on in the Lord. If you are in Pittsburgh or know of medical families in Pittsburgh that could use the support Side By Side-Pittsburgh can bring as described in this book, please send them our way.

Our website is https://sidebysidepittsburgh.weebly.com and our email is sidebysidepittsburgh@gmail.com.

Reena McCormick
Project Coordinator

REFERENCES

Keller, Timothy J., & Keller, Kathy. (2011). *The Meaning of Marriage: Facing the Complexities of Commitment with the Wisdom of God.* New York, NY: Penguin Group.

NOTES

NOTES

NOTES

Made in the USA
Monee, IL
20 May 2022

96820156R00079